PRACE FOR

The Mother-Daughter Legacy

The Mother-Daughter Legacy emphasizes the
special bond between mothers and daughters while
reminding us that the love we pour into this
moment is what is remembered.

Sandra P. Aldrich
Author, *Will I Ever Be Whole Again?* and *One Single Mother to Another*

The Mother-Daughter Legacy is a thoughtful book
that will inspire much reflection yet also lighten your
spirit with humorous incidents from the lives of the
authors. This book was particularly touching to me,
having lost a dear son-in-law just two months before
reading this manuscript. Reading Cara's journal
entries that deal with the loss of her mother were
particularly healing for me. *The Mother-Daughter Legacy*
will encourage mothers to realize how important
their input into their children's lives is and to
take heart at the thought of how rewarding it will
be to see their children grow into healthy,
loving and spiritual adults.

Anna Hayford
Wife of Pastor Jack W. Hayford

People say that as you grow older, you become your mother. How blessed am I! All my life I dreamed of someday having a daughter so that I could have the kind of relationship with my daughter that I have with my mother. Carole and Cara's book, *The Mother-Daughter Legacy,* reminds me that much of the fruit I desire for my own daughters will be a direct result of an abiding relationship with them and that the power of my words will, for better or worse, remain in their hearts.

Lisa Whelchel

Author, *The Facts of Life and Other Lessons My Father Taught Me*
and *Creative Correction*
Founder, MomTime Ministries

The Mother Daughter Legacy

Carole Lewis & Cara Symank

Regal

From Gospel Light
Ventura, California, U.S.A.

PUBLISHED BY REGAL BOOKS
FROM GOSPEL LIGHT
VENTURA, CALIFORNIA, U.S.A.
PRINTED IN THE U.S.A.

Regal Books is a ministry of Gospel Light, a Christian publisher dedicated to serving the local church. We believe God's vision for Gospel Light is to provide church leaders with biblical, user-friendly materials that will help them evangelize, disciple and minister to children, youth and families.

It is our prayer that this Regal book will help you discover biblical truth for your own life and help you meet the needs of others. May God richly bless you.

For a free catalog of resources from Regal Books/Gospel Light, please call your Christian supplier or contact us at 1-800-4-GOSPEL *or* www.regalbooks.com.

Cover and interior design by Robert Williams
Edited by Deena Davis

Library of Congress Cataloging-in-Publication Data

Lewis, Carole, 1942–
  The mother-daughter legacy / Carole Lewis and Cara Symank.
    p. cm.
  Includes bibliographical references.
  ISBN 0-8307-3335-3 (hardcover) 0-8307-3339-6 (paperback)
  1. Mothers and daughters—Religious aspects—Christianity. 2. Christian women—Religious life. 3. Lewis, Carole, 1942– 4. Symank, Cara. I. Symank, Cara. II. Title.
  BV4529.18.L49 2004
  248.8'43—dc22   2004002448

1   2   3   4   5   6   7   8   9   10   /   10   9   8   7   6   5   4

Rights for publishing this book in other languages are contracted by Gospel Light Worldwide, the international nonprofit ministry of Gospel Light. Gospel Light Worldwide also provides publishing and technical assistance to international publishers dedicated to producing Sunday School and Vacation Bible School curricula and books in the languages of the world. For additional information, visit www.gospellightworldwide.org; write to Gospel Light Worldwide, P.O. Box 3875, Ventura, CA 93006; or send an e-mail to info@gospellightworldwide.org.

Dedication

This book is lovingly dedicated to our moms and their lasting legacy of love. May we continue to pass on the legacy to our children and grandchildren, and may the legacy live on for a thousand generations.

Frances Juliet Caulk Harper
March 5, 1913–January 3, 2003
and
Shari Anne Lewis Symank
April 21, 1962–November 22, 2001

Know therefore that the LORD your God is God; he is the faithful God, keeping his covenant of love to a thousand generations of those who love him and keep his commands.

DEUTERONOMY 7:9

Contents

Foreword

As I turned the pages of this manuscript, I realized what a rare privilege I have had to know all four generations described in this rich and wonderful legacy. Try as I may, I cannot think of another family outside of my own bloodline about whom I could make such a claim. Come to think of it, the women in this book and I share a blood kinship thicker than any human tie. Our lives have been joined together through the blood of Jesus Christ.

Frances, the matriarch of this generational foursome, was in my Sunday School class for years. She and her friends were pushing 80 with all the gusto of schoolgirls. I taught the class—when they let me. God forbid that they should get their tickle boxes turned over about anything. Frances Harper was slap-knee hilarious, and neither I nor anyone else in that class could compete if she had a mind to take the stage. She affectionately wrapped everyone she knew around her little finger. She was a teacher's pet if I've ever had one. I called her Mammy because that's what her family called her. And Frances made everyone feel like family. I had the joy of celebrating her heavenly home going just as I had celebrated her life every time I had the pleasure of her company.

Carole, Frances's daughter, and the second-generation matriarch, is one of the best friends I've ever had. I don't have the time or space to share all the reasons why, so I'll just throw out a few. She is trustworthy. In a world where you don't know who you can trust, you can trust Carole. She is a loving straight talker, and I respect that. Carole is a born women's leader, though she'd be reluctant to admit it. All she's done is obey God. What He's done with her obedience is a bigger mystery to Carole than to anyone else. She and I have poured our lives into the same church for 20 years, joyfully spilling over into each other's ministries as often as we could splash. I have rarely known anyone to whom faith comes so easily. Carole Lewis trusts God. I've witnessed numerous prime opportunities for her to dissolve in doubt, but she simply will not do it. In a nutshell, I'm crazy about her.

Shari. Oh, Shari! This precious third-generation matriarch, Carole's middle child, was as dedicated to motherhood as any woman I've ever seen. Her day-in, day-out devotion to her three beautiful daughters was over the top. In most of our estimations, they had her nowhere near long enough. But if love is like peanut butter, Shari loved them such a heap that they have plenty left to spread out over the rest of their lives. She loved them more in those short years than many could in a century.

The day after Shari died, I lamented that I had not spent more time with her. She lived in a town outside the Houston area, and I saw her often as she attended Bible study or dropped by the church. I didn't know her nearly as well as I knew her mother. When I stopped by the funeral home to help plan the service, I was handed a stack of Bible studies that I'd written and Shari had completed. Her husband, Jeff, asked me to take a look at them in case they might have a bearing on what I felt led to share at the funeral. I held them like treasures against my heart and almost couldn't bear to read her private thoughts. Later that evening, when I had the courage to begin flipping through the pages, I saw countless places where I had asked a question in print and Shari had answered it in her own handwriting. Through a flood of tears, I realized that Shari and I had spent hours together. We shared the best kind of visits. Amid all those 10-week Bible studies, no fewer than hundreds of times and for countless hours, we met over God's Word.

Cara, Shari's eldest daughter, is the fourth generation of strong and loving women in this wonderful lineage. She mirrors all the best features of her predecessors.

I've had the privilege of watching Cara grow up—sometimes from across the aisle and sometimes from a distance. What a mighty fine job of growing up she has done. She is a very gifted young woman with an infectious smile that steals your heart in an instant. The dignity she has displayed after her mother's death is nothing less than astounding. Cara, her sisters and I have a bond that was anchored by depth more than length, however. I received a frantic call minutes after the freak accident that took Shari's life. Later I learned, and will always treasure, that Cara's youngest sister, knowing how "close" Shari and I had been through Bible study, insisted, "Beth Moore should be here!" And right she was. I jumped in the car, grabbed another good friend of the family and headed to the scene. It looked like a war zone.

I made it to the hospital right after Jesus had swept Shari into His arms. As I stole just a moment alone with her and brushed the hair out of her stilled face, I thought of how He had just been standing in that very room. I inhaled to see if His fragrance still lingered. We all remained in a waiting room for several hours before heading to our homes.

My daughter, Melissa, and I had the unspeakable privilege of spending the next several days with Shari's precious girls. We were with each other constantly, picking out clothes for the funeral, talking, crying, shopping and eating together. My most precious memory with them is one I would not be able to speak because I would never be able to get it out of my mouth without warbling sobs. I want to try to write it, however, because God used it to make such a point to me.

Some of us gathered at the church the morning before the funeral to have a private viewing. I assumed the girls had already been escorted in, but I soon learned that I was mistaken. The wife of our pastoral care minister, a good friend, came to me and said, "Beth, the girls are going in for the viewing now with their daddy. You need to go with them."

"Oh, Peggy, please don't make me. I can't stand it!"

"Yes, you can, Beth. The girls themselves invited you into this sacred time of loss, and you have no more important place to be than right beside them at the hardest point."

So I went.

It was just as hard as I thought it was going to be, but I learned a lesson I'll never forget. Being side by side to celebrate and to mourn is what life in the family of God is all about. It's what love is all about. Those few minutes I shared with the girls and their father were some of the most sacred, intimate moments of my life. Though they were understandably oblivious to my presence right behind them, I knew I was right where God wanted me—in their shadow and in His. I knew that if they could bear the loss, I could bear to stand nearby. Pain itself does not kill us. Sometimes, in fact, it's a reminder that we're still very much alive. Still risking love, still taking the time, still acting like family.

So when I tell you I have known the women in this book, I do not exaggerate. We have shared some real life. You don't have to know them to share in their experiences. If you're a mother or a daughter, in countless ways you already have shared common experiences. Certain things are delightful commonalities of the feminine gender. As Carole and Cara tell their stories, they invite you to remember yours and frame it in the certain faithfulness of God.

You might consider also leaving a written legacy to be treasured in the generations to come. Has God been faithful? Tell the next generation! Build a heritage of faith, dear one. Nothing is more priceless nor at times more expensive. Life is worth living. Do it with everything you have, and then pass it on.

I will utter hidden things, things from of old—
what we have heard and known, what our
fathers have told us. We will not hide them
from their children; we will tell the next generation the praiseworthy deeds of the LORD, his
power, and the wonders he has done. So the
next generation would know them, even the
children yet to be born, and they in turn would
tell their children. Then they would put their
trust in God and would not forget his deeds
(Ps. 78:2-4,6-7).

Beth Moore
Author and Bible Teacher

Shari's Legacy

Thanksgiving Day of 2001 seemed to be much like any other, but ultimately it proved to be unlike any that our family had experienced before or (I hope) will ever experience again.

Johnny and I had invited our family to our house for lunch, and all but our oldest daughter, Lisa, had gathered there. Lisa, Kent and their two children had gone to Kent's grandmother's farm for the day.

The end of the fall First Place session was drawing near, and my daughter Shari, who had been in my class that session, brought a sugar-free pumpkin pie so that the two of us would have a healthy dessert. After lunch, Shari, having started this tradition at least 10 years before, began decorating my Christmas tree. Because we live on a bay, we put up a nautical tree filled with fishnet swags, buoys and sailboats. Shari lovingly wrapped each branch with lights. Just before 4:00 P.M., Shari's husband, Jeff, came into the room to tell her they needed to leave for his parents' home. Shari said, "Just a minute; I'm almost through," as she put the last ornament on the tree and stepped back to see if everything was perfect. The rest of the story took place a few hours later.

After having dinner with Jeff's family, Shari, Jeff and their three girls were preparing to drive home. All five were in the car when Shari remembered some things she wanted to give to Jeff's mom. Shari jumped out of the car and went to the back of their Expedition where she retrieved the items. While Shari and Jeff's mom stood behind the car talking, a car suddenly left the street and headed down the sidewalk toward them. Just before impact, the car swerved, hit a light pole and ricocheted back into Shari, throwing her into the yard.

Back at our house, Johnny and two of his brothers were sitting outside on the patio, talking. I was tired and had gone to bed early. About 9:15 P.M., I was awakened by a call from my granddaughter Cara. She was screaming something about her mother, and I couldn't make any sense of what she was saying. I kept trying to get her to slow down and tell me what was happening. I didn't comprehend until Ronnie, Cara's uncle, took the phone and told me that a car driven by an inebriated teenager had hit Shari. An ambulance had taken Shari to the medical center, and the situation didn't look good.

I went outside to tell Johnny that something terrible had happened and that we had to go to the hospital immediately. On the drive into town, I called Lisa at the farm, and she and her family immediately started the drive home. Lisa was at least three hours away, so we decided she should go straight to our house to wait with my mom and Johnny's brothers.

When we arrived at the hospital an hour later, Shari was in surgery. We were gathered in the family room at the hospital when the chaplain came in to tell us that Shari was gone.

Shari was our middle child. In birth order she was sandwiched between our eldest, Lisa, and our baby, John. Shari was a typical middle child in many ways. She always seemed to have more emotional needs than the other two and was a mama's girl most of her life. I still don't know if she really needed more help with her homework than our other two or if she just needed more of my attention. I will be forever grateful for the many hours I spent reading to Shari books that she needed to read for school. She said she understood them better if I read them to her. I treasure the memory of the night when I became engrossed in the book I was reading to Shari—only to look over and see her sleeping! It wasn't funny at the time, but now I love the memory. It was so Shari.

She loved babies even while she was still a baby herself. She was only 19 months old when John was born, but she was a natural mother even then. As she grew older, she wanted nothing more than to be married and have her own babies. She said to me many times, "I sure hope the Lord doesn't come back before I can have babies." Shari truly believed that being a wife and mother was the reason God placed her on this earth.

Shari's behavior with her first child, Cara, reminds me of when I played with dolls as a child. Since Shari changed Cara's clothes every time a spot appeared on them, and she took pictures of each outfit after the change, it seemed as if she took pictures of Cara all day long. Cara had so many pictures taken of her that she would break into a grin whenever she saw a camera!

Shari became so adept at taking pictures of her family that she could take great pictures of everything. When she went to the Holy Land with us in 1997, she took the most beautiful picture of the Garden Tomb. It was so gorgeous that she entered it in a photography contest and won first place.

Shari's photo of the Garden Tomb

Shari loved special occasions. She took great care to make birthdays and holidays special for the people she loved. I guess the most difficult holiday for me was the first Christmas without Shari. Jeff and the girls had asked me to spend the night with them on Christmas Eve so that they wouldn't have to be alone Christmas morning. After watching the girls open gifts that Shari had wrapped early, I was heartbroken to think she would never wrap another gift for Jeff or her girls.

Cara was 19, Christen, 15 and Amanda, 13 when Shari was taken from their lives. When Bible teacher Beth Moore told the girls at Shari's memorial service, "Girls, you had more Momma in the years you had her than half the people in this room when they bury their mommas at 90 years old," I began to think about the legacy of love that Shari left to her three daughters, which will continue to play out as they grow older.

This book was conceived and written as a result of our family's having been jolted into the realization that life is uncertain at best and that many of us will be snatched from this world before our loved ones are ready for us to leave. Losing Shari has been a journey of unspeakable pain and joy—pain at the loss of her presence in our lives and joy in watching God work on our behalf.

My granddaughter Cara began writing about the loss of her mother in the months following Shari's death. As we shared our thoughts, God birthed the idea of this book about the legacy that mothers pass on to their children and, specifically, the legacies that our mothers passed on to us.

The Mother-Daughter Legacy is a tribute to mothers everywhere. Cara and I pray that each of you will be encouraged by our stories to want to do the best job of mothering possible every day of your life.

The Importance of a Legacy

When I was a young wife and mother of three small children under the age of four, my days were consumed with the demands of caring for my family. I fell into bed each night knowing that the next day would be much like the day before. Sunday mornings were especially busy as we prepared to go to church.

It was on one of these Sunday mornings that I was vividly reminded of the importance of legacy. My Sunday School teacher, Sammie Buchanan, said, "When your children grow up, they will never remember if the house was clean or even what they had for dinner; but they will remember if their mother read to them or prayed with them every day."

That simple statement changed my life. No longer did I feel guilty if I sat and read to my children when laundry needed to be folded. I began to play with my children instead of sending them out to play. We snuggled in bed at night to read Bible stories, even when the floor was cluttered with toys that needed to be picked up.

A legacy of love is something that every mother wants to leave her child. Most of us miss the mark more than we hit it; but God, in His mercy and grace, makes up for our deficiencies by gently guiding us and showing us the way. I am forever grateful for a Sunday School teacher who pointed the way for me to carry on my mom's legacy. Mom always had time for me and loved me unconditionally, just because I was her child.

I was the younger of two daughters born seven years apart. My mother was not blessed with sons, so her perception of motherhood was somewhat skewed. She honestly believed that every woman should have a daughter. Her philosophy was that daughters, even when grown, would stay close to family, whereas sons would grow up, marry and leave. I grew up hearing this philosophy and heard it repeated at the birth of each baby in our family. Mom loved her grandsons just as much as she did her granddaughters, and she never played favorites; but she loved little girls and believed that every mom should have at least one daughter.

On January 3, 2003, Mom left her earthly body and joined her Lord and Savior Jesus Christ in heaven. Mom died two months short of her ninetieth birthday. My daughter Lisa was at her side. I was in California with my husband, Johnny, for his medical treatment, when my mother took her last breath. I called Lisa to see what kind of night Mom had spent, and Lisa said, "Oh, Momma! Mammy danced into heaven at 6:30 this morning." My mom died as she had lived—dancing.

There is a special bond between mothers and daughters that cannot be explained. A daughter learns how to be a wife and mother from her mom's example; her mom learned from her mother, and the legacy lives on from mother to daughter, generation after generation.

Carole and her mother, Frances Harper (photographer: Norma Williams)

As I share remembrances of my mom, I want to pass on her legacy of love to my children, who in turn will pass it on to their children. I wish the same for you as you consider the legacy your mother gave you and the one that you are passing on.

This book is a tribute to mothers and daughters everywhere and to the legacy of love that is in their power to give to the next generation. My prayer for you, as you read this book, is that you will see your life through the eyes of your children and that you will endeavor, from this day forward, to be a living legacy of love to them and to your children's children.

CHAPTER ONE

The Legacy of Nurture

Moms come in all shapes and sizes, but that doesn't matter to their daughters. Little girls, from the earliest age, want to talk like Mom, dress like Mom and be like Mom. Even girls who have been abused want to stay with Mom, always hoping for a better life.

Girls love their moms—just because.

Moms wield a greater influence on their daughters' lives than any other person. Sometimes daughters want to change things about themselves that they didn't like in their moms, only to find that when they are grown, they are very much like their moms in many ways.

Moms who did not receive the right kind of love from their mothers often replicate that deficiency with their daughter's rearing, and a love-hate relationship forms. Nevertheless, a daughter never stops wishing and hoping for her mom's unconditional love.

The mom who nurtures her child leaves a legacy of nurturing that will continue from generation to generation.

My earliest remembrances were that my mom always wanted me around. I never felt as if I were a bother or an imposition. My mother's nurturing nature continued after she had grandchildren and great-grandchildren.

Nothing was ever too much trouble if it involved being with her family.

From the time I was very small, my mom and I took train trips to see her parents in Kansas City, Missouri. It was quite natural when I had children of my own to want the same experience for them. When my children were four, six and eight, Mom, my three kids and I drove back to Kansas City with my aunt, my mom's sister, who had been visiting us in Houston. We stayed with my aunt a few days and then rode the train back to Houston so that the kids could experience an overnight train ride.

Shari and her
daughter Cara, 1982

When my daughter Shari's eldest, Cara, was born in 1982, my aunt and uncle still lived in Kansas City. They were closing their antiques business and planned to sell everything at an auction, so Mom, Shari, two-month-old Cara and I flew to Kansas City for a few days and had the most wonderful time. I'll never forget how Shari reacted to the fall foliage. Because she had grown up in Houston, Shari had never seen the seasons change. In Houston, most of the leaves fall off the trees before they ever change colors. During our stay in Kansas City, we stopped the car many times so that Shari could take pictures of the beautiful red, orange and yellow leaves.

The trip to Kansas City and the antiques auction fueled Shari and me to the point that we opened a small antiques shop inside a tearoom when Cara was eight months old. We each worked every other day, and I kept Cara the days that Shari worked. Cara spent much of her infancy at antiques auctions with her mom and me.

The legacy of nurture from my mom to me and then to Shari is so powerful that Cara has naturally taken on the nurturing role left vacant when Shari died. Cara would think nothing of driving home from college to take her sisters shopping or to go somewhere with her dad and sisters. Nurturing is something that is hard to pinpoint, but it is my belief that a well-nurtured child believes that he or she is so special that everyone always wants them around. When you've experienced the love of a nurturing mother, it becomes so much easier to believe that God feels the same way about you and always wants to be with you.

Cara wrote a wonderful story about what it means to have a nurturing mom.

Cara Symank

Look at the birds of the air; they do not sow or reap or store away in barns, and yet your heavenly Father feeds them. Are you not much more valuable than they? Who of you by worrying can add a single hour to his life?
MATTHEW 6:26-27

As a small child, I wanted answers from my mother. By the time I was a teenager, I felt that I had been given enough answers. As I changed, my mother's ways of conveying that she cared for me changed. Despite the fact that my sisters and I varied in age, Mom was able to tailor her caring ways to our individual understanding.

At the end of my sophomore year in high school, my mother had the privilege of taking a trip to Israel and walking the same ground as our Lord and Savior Jesus Christ. I was a little worried that something would happen to her while she was gone, but fear was not my foremost emotion. I was exceedingly happy that she had been given the opportunity to travel to a land where she would be able to see things such as the tomb in which Jesus had been buried. Just before she left, my mother gave each of us—Christen, Amanda and me—a box. Inside were a few small gifts and a card for each day that she would be gone. Every day I went to my box and found one of her handwritten notes. Sometimes it was a note of encouragement, perhaps about the final exam I was to take that day, or simply a short sentence that said she was missing me and thinking about me.

At age 15, I did not realize the depth of love and care that my mom put into her every action. Everything she did mirrored her fundamental beliefs, and the boxes that overflowed with encouragement were a perfect example. When she was here enjoying life with the rest of us, my mother's love for my sisters and me was something I had grown accustomed to. I incessantly soaked in Momma; therefore, I thought very little of life's being any other way. Now that I am older, and without my mother's constant display of encouragement, I realize that each act of her kindness was done with special thought.

A journal entry written by my mother sparked my memory of the boxes she left behind for my sisters and me when she went to Israel.

From the time I heard of it [the trip to Israel] last fall, something inside of me was saying that would be an awesome thing. Can you imagine walking on the same ground the Israelites walked, much less where Jesus was born and died? But the "me" part of me kicked in. What about my safety? I have three little kids I must raise. This is not my idea of vacation. The Middle East—I watch the news—no thanks! Why not Hawaii? Besides, we're broke!

I have continually asked God to remove this desire to seek this out if it wasn't about Him. Well, it's not going away. It's only growing stronger. What does He want to teach me or show me? I don't know; but from experience I am learning that as hard as it is to do what He says, it's even harder not to. He is also showing me that when I get my focus right, He will provide. How would I explain to Amanda, who is scared in Chappell Hill, that Mom's going to the Middle East? He will provide a way to do what He has asked me to do—that's the way He's been doing it forever.

As I read those words, I realized something. First and foremost, my mother gave us those cards of encouragement because she was concerned that we would be in fear of her safety while she was gone. She wanted to make sure that any distress the three of us might be feeling would be replaced with her words of encouragement. Second, I discovered that she was fearful of leaving, because there might be a chance that something would happen to her, and my sisters and I would be left without a mother. We can learn a great lesson from my mother about the uselessness of worrying. As she left my grandparents' house on Thanksgiving night of 2001, she felt no anxiety about the possibility of her life coming to an end. However, without warning, it did end. She was not given a spare moment to worry about how those of us remaining were going to make it without her; her heavenly Father simply called her home, and she went! Why should any of us let fear hold us back from the things we know God has called us to do, which in my mother's case was to travel to Israel? God's timing will always prevail, whether someone chooses to worry or not!

I am grateful that my mother was the godly woman that she was to my sisters and me. Even though while she was alive I didn't see the fullness of the blessing I had been given, it is now quite evident that she gave each of us so very much.

Moms everywhere love to say, "Well, I did the best I could," when talking about their relationships with their children. My answer to that statement is "Not a good answer!" I know that I didn't always do the best that I could! Many times, I knew in my heart that I could do better.

If nurturing doesn't come easily for you, for whatever reason, you can still learn to nurture your children. As author Zig Ziglar says, "It is easier to a act your way into a new way of feeling than to feel your way into a new way of acting."[1] A nurturing legacy to your children will leave a God-sized imprint on their hearts. Proverbs 22:6 says, "Train a child in the way he should go, and when he is old he will not turn from it." This is a legacy-making verse if we can learn the value of nurturing our children, who are a gift from God.

LEAVING A LEGACY

Each one of us has daily opportunities to leave a legacy of nurture to those we love. It might be as simple as speaking an encouraging word, writing a handwritten note or giving a big hug as you say "I love you" to your child.

- What can you do to make your daughter feel special and loved?
- How can you encourage your daughter in an area that is difficult for her?
- What about your daughter makes you very proud of her? Share it with her.

Note

1. Zig Ziglar, *See You at the Top* (New York: Pelican Publishing Company, 1975), p. 238.

CHAPTER TWO

The Legacy of Family

The legacy of a loving family is truly the gift that keeps on giving. All of my growing-up years we lived in Houston, far away from extended family. For the most part, family celebrations, such as birthdays and holidays, were just the four of us—Mom, Dad, my sister, Glenda, and me.

The legacy of family became larger than life after my sister and I were grown and had children of our own. We celebrated every holiday and birthday together. We had grown to a nice-sized family of 12, and with birthdays spread throughout the year, our entire family spent many happy times together. Although our children wanted to have birthday parties with their friends, they always made it clear that those parties were not to take the place of our family parties.

After my children and my sister's children married and had children of their own, our family exploded from nice-sized to gigantic, with as many as 31 people at our family gatherings if everyone was present.

My parents built a second home on Galveston Bay after Johnny and I married, so many of our family celebrations were spent at their bay house. Forty years later, Johnny and I live on Galveston Bay, just five streets from my parents' bay house, and many of our family celebrations are held in our home.

My daughters, Lisa and Shari, planned all the summer birthdays around my travel schedule, because family was such an important part of our lives. Consequently, I never missed a family birthday for any of our children or grandchildren. This is pretty amazing when you consider how many family members we have.

Someone outside of our family may think this is too much togetherness, but our family believes that by celebrating birthdays and holidays, we make time to be together that otherwise probably wouldn't happen.

Last year, our first year without Shari, our family didn't feel much like partying. We found ourselves combining three months of birthdays into one party. After one of these parties, I realized how much we all missed Shari and how she would have never let this happen. Shari believed that every person's birthday was special enough to have its own celebration. If we did celebrate two birthdays together, such as Christen's and Katherine's, just 11 days apart, then we always had two separate cakes so that each girl could blow out her own candles.

The legacy of family starts at birth. Here is one of Cara's earliest remembrances of her mom.

Cara Symank

At the age of two, I smiled from ear to ear in amazement as I watched my mother enthusiastically jump up and down as she sang the song I would be singing at my first ballet recital. The scene is vividly etched in my memory. We stood in the living room, on the stark orange carpet, bouncing up and down and singing about poodles:

> We are dancing poodles, and we are proud to
>   say—
> we come from France, we love to dance, we
>   always do ballet.

As I reflected back on this particular moment so long ago, I thought, *There we were, bouncing around and acting as if we didn't have a care in the world.* Then it struck me. At the age of two, the idea of getting up on stage in front of a large crowd of people was my biggest care in the world. My mother had not enthusiastically bounced around for the sheer fun of it; she had done it to convey to me that what I cared about mattered to her. Sorting through the memories of my mother, I realized that one main principle sustained me throughout the course of our time together: Though my challenges varied throughout the years, the greatness or smallness of the tasks was insignificant because of the simple fact that what was important to me was important to my mom.

I never dreamed that I would be sitting here today catching only glimpses of the relationship between my mother and me, rather than living it out. While growing up, my family consisted of my mother, my father and my two younger sisters, Christen and Amanda. As far as I was concerned, the five of us were going to remain a family until the end of time. Unforeseen to each of us was the death of my mother at the age of 39 as a result of the decision made by an 18-year-old girl to drive while intoxicated.

Although my heart has experienced great sorrow at the loss of my mother, when I reflect on the amazing times we were able to have together, I am thankful. She did an incredible job of raising my sisters and me during the time she was given to do so. Although I am certain that she had her regrets, as every mother does, she had no reason to fret that her mistakes would ever outweigh her unconditional love and support that so radiated our lives. Proverbs 31:28 says, "Her children arise and call her blessed." This is how the children of a woman of noble character describe her: blessed. My mother was blessed. My mother lived as if each day was the most important day, and she continually instilled solid truths in us with deep tenderness.

I recall thinking from the time I was a very small child that my mother could do absolutely anything. Watching her caused me to long for my own opportunity to be a mother. By the age of six, I was stuffing dolls under my shirt and looking at myself sideway in the bathroom mirror. I had seen my mother's stomach grow two times, and I began to dream of the day that mine would do the same.

One day, in complete dismay, I stood across from my mother in the bathroom and said, as best as I can remember, "Mom, how do I get from here to there?"

"What do you mean, Cara?"

"Well, you are my mom, but how did you get to be my mom? Were you ever little, or will I always be little and you always be big?"

I remember her smile as she said, "Of course I was little. I was a little girl just like you."

"So then, how do I get from here to there?"

"Well, you get older every time you have a birthday, and one day you will be my age and have babies of your own."

"Yeah, but you keep having birthdays, too, so you'll get older and then I can never catch up with you."

I vividly recall her saying nothing in return, yet smiling at me as if I were life's greatest purpose.

I continued, "So, how did you get to know all this stuff? Does it just happen? You just get big, and then you know everything?"

She gently replied, "You'll know when you get here."

I am now just six years younger than the age that my mother was on the day I asked her how it was that she got to know everything. I am trusting that one must learn a whole lot between the ages of 20 and 26, because after all, she told me that I would know when I got there!

Inquiring about how to get from here to there was only one of the many questions I wanted answers to as a small child. I can't imagine actually caring about the answers to some of my questions at that age, but I asked; and to this day I still remember the answers I was given. True, my mother spent a large portion of one-on-one time with me during the day while my father was at work, but some of my questions were a two-person job that required my father's help. He usually held me close on his lap while my mother gave answers.

The explanation of eternity was no doubt a two-person task when I asked about it at the age of six or seven. There I went, charging through the living room, just missing the end of the couch, and making a bee-line for my mother and father, who were sitting in the playroom that looked out through French doors to the backyard. I sat there for a moment listening to bits and pieces of their conversation as I thought about the topic that had been bothering me all day long: *What happens if I don't want to be around for all eternity?* I waited just long enough to be acknowledged before I sprang my question.

"Okay. So when you die, you go to heaven where you live forever. So, really, you don't ever die, right?"

"Yes," my mother said. "When we leave this earth, we will go to heaven to be with Jesus, and that is where we will be forever."

"But . . . so, when does forever end? Does it ever end?" I said, starting to get a little worked up.

My mother smiled and looked over to my father as if she might need some help. I remember the smile he gave in return as she said, "No, honey, there is no end once we get to heaven; but you will want to be in heaven."

I interrupted before she was able to continue, "Yeah, but not forever."

"Why not forever?"

By this time I was beginning to tear up. "Because!"

"Cara, it's okay. Listen, you like being on Earth, right? You have fun playing, right? Have you ever wanted this to end?"

Wiping my tears I quickly answered, "No." I bet that for a moment she was relieved until she realized that I had only taken a breath before replying, "But that's different."

She brushed my bangs away from my face and gently continued to help me understand. "Cara, sweetie, it's going to be okay. Eternity is something that is hard for any of us to understand. It scared me, too, when I was little, but now I'm not scared anymore."

Apparently she had spoken the right combination of words. I sat in silence for a moment as I rubbed my eyes and my nose. "Well," I said, "do you think maybe if I ask Jesus if I can just sleep for a little bit, He'll let me—'cause I might get bored after a long time?"

Once again, pushing my bangs back as she smiled a soft half smile, she said, "I bet you can ask Him."

Whether or not my mother knew how much I valued such answers, I did. Deep down, I believe that she knew exactly how valuable her time and patience were to me as her child. Had she not known, I doubt that she would have always taken the time to give me gentle answers that I was able to understand.

I dearly love my family, and I get anxious to see them if it has been a while since we were last together. I can fully understand what my mom meant when she would say, "You and Johnny might move away, but you are not taking those kids with you!" She was teasing, but with those words she was telling me how precious my children were to her.

Family relationships sometimes become strained, because even though we love each other, we also know each other better than anyone else in the world. For this reason, we must learn how to relate to each person in our family as God relates to us. God gives us some great advice in Hebrews 10:24-25 that certainly applies to our families: "And let us consider how we may spur one another on toward love and good deeds. Let us not give up meeting together, as some are in the habit of doing, but let us encourage one another—and all the more as you see the Day approaching." Although the larger meaning of this verse is about believers meeting together, we can apply this concept to our family life, too. There will come a day when we will no longer have a conscious influence on our family, so it is imperative that we learn the legacy of family unity and love today.

Family legacies are precious indeed. I pray with so many women at conferences and retreats who are brokenhearted because of the strife and dissension in their families—sometimes their family members go years without speaking to one another.

If there is estrangement in your family, start praying that God will put the broken pieces back together again. God might even want you to be the one who picks up the phone today to start the healing process. When a family member dies, the entire family mourns the loss. The loss is felt to an even greater extent when there are unresolved hurts and pain. Life is just too short to spend a single day separated from your family.

LEAVING A LEGACY

If your family legacy is not all that you wish it were, you can begin to change what it is to what you would like it to be. Here are some suggestions to start the process:

- Pray that God will heal the hurts of the past and restore unity in your family. Keep praying that prayer every day, and don't give up!

- Send a note or a gift to begin the healing process.
- Ask God to break the chain of dissension in your immediate family so that your children do not suffer as you have.

CHAPTER THREE

The Legacy
of Example

Like most children, I took my childhood for granted. It was not until after I became a Christian, when I was 12, that I read Luke 12:48: "And from the one who has been entrusted with much, much more will be asked." I knew that this verse was meant for me and that God would expect more from me than He would from a person who had endured a tortured childhood.

As I have reflected on some of my mom's attributes, I realize that many of them were naturally passed on to me and in turn passed on to my children. Without even realizing it, *who we are* speaks much more loudly than *what we say*. Children are blessed when they have parents who live out a loving legacy by setting a loving example to follow.

DISCIPLINE

My childhood was a simple one. I had two parents who loved God, each other and their girls, in that order. Life was easy, with few rules. The only hard-and-fast rule I can remember was that I was not allowed to talk back to Mom. That meant that I wasn't allowed to argue with her, roll my eyes or even make faces when I wanted my own way. From my earliest remembrance, when my mom was displeased with me, she would begin to bite her lower lip and say, "You'd better straighten up and fly right." Looking back, I had no idea what those words actually meant, but I knew then that I had better start behaving myself.

This legacy was obviously passed on to me! When Pat, my assistant at First Place, read this part of the book, she said, "Carole, you also bite your lower lip when you are upset."

Speaking of discipline, I didn't receive many spankings as a child. I probably would have received more, but my dad always rescued me. I remember one day when we were getting ready to go somewhere—my mom had dressed me and then began to get herself dressed. I went outside and rode my bike through a mud puddle, splashing mud all over my dress, shoes and socks. When I rode up to the house, my dad was outside and saw what had happened. He took one look and said, "I'll go inside with you, and we'll tell Mom together."

In elementary school, children were chosen to be hall monitors, restroom monitors and classroom monitors. One day, when I entered the restroom, the restroom monitor had gone into one of the stalls, leaving her shoes outside by the chair where she sat to monitor our behavior. I thought it would be funny to throw her shoes out the bathroom window. The only problem was that one of the shoes broke the window, and I found myself in the principal's office. The principal gave me a stern lecture about this incident now being a part of my permanent record, telling me that nothing like this had better happen again. I had to tell my mom when I got home. She felt I had been punished enough by having to go to the principal's office and didn't hand out a further reprimand.

I began driving a car in 1956. I was 14 and already had my permanent license. One day, instead of hitting the brake, I hit the gas pedal and drove the car right through the garage wall into the kitchen! My mom was cooking dinner, and I had a pretty good idea she was going to be angry when I went inside. As I opened the door, I turned on the tears and told Mom how it wasn't my fault, because my foot slipped and hit the gas pedal. I remember my dad walking into the kitchen from the den, saying, "That's no problem; I can fix it." Crisis over, discussion ended.

Another time, when I was out driving the car, I drove through our neighbor's yard. It had been raining, and the car's tires left deep trenches in the neighbor's grass. I went into our house and started crying, telling my dad what I had done. He said, "I'll go over there with you, and we'll tell Mr. Eckhart together what you did." We walked over to the neighbor's house, and I told Mr. Eckhart that I had trenched his yard. He just laughed and said, "I'll have Rusty [his son] fix it tomorrow."

I only skipped school one time in my life. I was in the tenth grade, and I went with Johnny and another couple to pay a speeding ticket Johnny had received. We drove up to Bellville, Texas, about an hour from home, to pay the ticket. We were back by noon. The next three hours until school was over were the longest three hours of my life. We went over to the other girl's house and made some guacamole salad. As soon as school was over at 3:00 P.M., I went straight home, told my mother what I had done and how sorry I was. Her only reprimand was, "Don't ever do that again."

The next time I wanted to skip school was during the same year on Senior Skip Day. All the high school seniors had gone swimming at a country club and left the rest of us at school. I called my mom and told her that some friends and I wanted to leave school and go swimming. She granted permission, and we left school at lunchtime. The only problem was that one of the other girls had not gotten permission. So when the school called home asking why she had not come back after lunch, we all got caught. The next week I went before the drill team's senior officers: My punishment was to sit out for the first two games the next year, ensuring that I would not letter in my junior year. Even though my mom and dad were not strict disciplinarians, I always had to take my lumps. My parents did not go to the school to try and get me out of trouble.

Why do I tell you these stories? To let you know that my view of God was shaped and molded early on from my experiences with my earthly mother and father. As I look back on my parents' form of discipline, or lack thereof, I have thought much about what I learned. I learned that I could go to God (my heavenly Father), knowing that He could fix any mess I made in life. I learned that God loves me unconditionally, as my parents did. My concept of God as a loving and caring Father who always wants the best for me is the reason that I have been able to accept my husband's cancer and my daughter's death. I also learned what God's mercy and grace look like. God has never given me justice—He has never given me the punishment I truly deserved. He has filtered my life and its circumstances through His loving hands.

The downside of my parents' leniency is that I grew up thinking that God would take my sin lightly, as my parents had done. I relegated God to the role of an indulgent parent instead of clearly seeing His holiness and righteousness and that He had rules (spelled out in His Word) that were intended to keep me safe. Where others might think of God as cruel, harsh or uncaring, I always felt (and feel) love and acceptance from His hand. I believe this is a direct result of feeling love and acceptance from my earthly parents.

I can't tell you with complete authority what the perfect discipline is for a child. My best guess is that it would include a balance of love and rules—not so many rules about right and wrong behavior that the child feels powerless, but enough consistency that the child learns whatever rules are needed.

CHORES

My mom did not teach me to do chores because she loved to do things for me. Some of the things we think are so important today were not important to my mom. Because Mom did not work outside the home, it was not important to her that I make my bed every day. I made it if I felt like it. If I didn't make it, the bed was always made when I got home from school. I remember my grandmother teaching me the proper way to make a bed when she visited from California. My dad's mother was a nurse, and she taught me how to properly square the corners of the sheets. I never forgot her lesson, and today I still make the bed the way she taught me to do it.

I did not wash or iron clothes while living at home. Consequently, when I was a young mom with three small children, I would get overwhelmed with the amount of ironing (in those days we didn't have permanent press). There was a woman in our neighborhood who had six children. She did ironing for five cents a piece to bring in extra money. Many times I took her three baskets of ironing so that the girls could wear a dress again before they outgrew it.

I did not learn to sew. My mom started to sew when she was nine years old; she told me that she had made clothes for a neighbor's baby while she was still a child herself. In fact, as I grew older and wanted to learn to sew, Mom would say, "Honey, run the vacuum cleaner for me, and I'll sew for you."

After I was grown, I asked Mom why she hadn't made me do household chores, and she said, "Honey, I knew you would have a lifetime to do all those things, and I was there to do them for you." My mom was the baby of eight children, and I'm sure that influenced her easy style of parenting with me. I also realize now that my sister was gone from home during my teenaged years, and Mom only had me at home.

Mom said that her dad made sure that all his children learned to play a musical instrument. He would listen to the children practice while he shaved in the morning and go in with shaving cream all over his face to make corrections when needed. As the baby, my mom was supposed to learn piano, but she said it didn't take long before her stern father let her quit. Like mother, like daughter. I took piano lessons for seven years but never became really good at playing piano because I never practiced enough.

I remember that when I was a child of 11 or 12, my parents would sometimes leave the house on Saturday mornings to run errands. I loved to hurry and clean the entire house while they were gone so that they would be proud of me when they returned. Because I never had to do chores, I thought of chores as fun activities I could do to surprise my parents.

Some of you may be shaking your heads at my lack of assigned responsibility. Some of you may have had a childhood similar to mine. Whichever style you are leaving as a legacy for your children, the key is balance. Discipline and the care of our possessions and home are a real part of life until the day we die, so we need to train our children with important life skills while letting them remain as carefree as possible.

After I was grown, with children of my own, it was hard to be consistent in teaching them to do chores. I found myself with three children under the age of four and a house full of toys and laundry. It was easier for me to send the kids out to play and do the work myself than to teach them what I had not learned to do as a child. If I had not worked outside the home when they were teens, I probably would have continued the same way I was taught and done everything myself.

Again, balance is the key. It's best not to shelter our kids from effort simply because they have a lifetime of work ahead of them.

I am grateful for a husband who taught our children to work. I believe they were better equipped for the "dailiness" of life for having learned how to clean house, do laundry and take care of the yard.

Although your legacy to your children contains both the good and the less than good, depending on what you were taught as a child, you can still learn to give balance to that legacy if you simply remember that everything you model for your children, every single day, contributes to the people they will become.

PEACE

One of the greatest legacies a mom can pass down to her children is the legacy of peace in the home. My own personality is the same as my mom's—fun loving but needing to be in control. Even though Mom had a stronger personality than Dad, I never observed her using her strength against him. I can honestly say that Mom and Dad never argued much. Dad came from a home where his parents fought constantly, and he determined that he and my mom would not repeat that legacy. Of course, there were disagreements, but nothing that lasted for any length of time.

My mom never nagged my dad about anything, and she passed that legacy on to me. I have come to realize this is a rare legacy indeed. I have friends who have shared with me that the habit of nagging was one they observed growing up, and they got married believing this is the way married couples interact.

Moms, if you consistently nag your husband, it is a strong probability that your daughter will continue this legacy when she gets married. On the other hand, the legacy of a peaceful home is a desirable one to leave.

CONSISTENCY

In the eighth grade, I wanted to take ballroom dancing lessons. All my friends were taking lessons, and I did everything to convince my mom that I needed to take lessons or my life would surely be ruined. My mom not only said no, but she also included the reason: "You may dance, but I'll never pay to teach you how." At the time, I thought her reason was the dumbest reason anyone could give. I realized later that my mom didn't want me to go dancing in undesirable places after I was grown. She was not going to pay money to help me get good at something she felt I didn't need to be doing.

I think the great thing my mom taught me was that her yes meant yes and her no meant no. I knew what my boundaries were, and because of that, I felt secure.

Isn't it the same way with God? He wants us to be able to do so many wonderful things, and He provides for most of our wants and all of our needs. He says no, but only when He knows that something might bring us harm.

HOSPITALITY

My mom loved to entertain. My earliest remembrances are of people at our house for dinner or for parties. I didn't realize until many years later that Mom passed on the legacy of hospitality to me just by her example and by my observation of how much fun she had when entertaining people in her home. Many of my friends, who do not entertain easily, tell me that their moms never entertained guests. Entertaining others is definitely something that is caught rather than taught.

I passed on this legacy to my own daughters. Early on they both showed a love of hospitality because they grew up helping to plan and prepare for parties. Lisa and Shari helped their dad cook the meals at Round Top, Texas, for our First Place F.O.C.U.S Weeks. Eventually, Lisa took over the job, and Shari helped her with the cooking. Lisa prepared the lunches at her children's Christian school for a number of years when they were in elementary school.

Cara's letter to her mom beautifully sums up the legacy of example.

Cara Symank

A Letter to Mom

June 2, 2003

Dear Mom,

I think a lot about what I would say to you if given the chance to speak to you for only a short time. This morning, as I was driving, I decided that I would tell you the simple things, because it's the simple things that I miss so much about you. I would thank you for being real and for raising the girls and me the way that you did. This morning, I kept visualizing what life would be like to have you here, just to have you back. I was thinking that if I could have you back, we would not even have to make up for lost time; we could just start from today. I quickly realized that now that you are in heaven, you are better than ever and happier than ever and that God knew that we were only going to be given the amount of time that we had with you. You were absolutely amazing, Mom. You were real, and you raised each of us to be the same. If I could tell you "Thank you" for that, I would. You instilled so much in me, and I am reaching a point where I can see so much of you coming out in me, which I love, because I think that you were an amazing mother. I only hope that I can give my children everything that you gave the girls and me. The values that you taught me are permanent, and I am truly grateful. I would also thank you for choosing Dad. The older I get, the more I realize that Dad is a man with a depth of character that most men know nothing about. I will strive to marry a man that will measure up to the one you chose. He is absolutely wonderful, and he is helping us every single step of the way. He refuses to give up on us. Mom, it has been a battle without you, yet our home is not void of smiles. We are getting better and better every day, but we will never ever forget you, and the pain of your absence will never completely dissipate. I miss you, Mom, and I love you.

Love,

"Sue" (Cara)

I can echo Cara's thoughts about example. Now that my mom is no longer with me, I've done a lot of thinking about what I learned from her. Even though I sometimes wish she had been a little stricter with me, in my heart of hearts I know that given my strong personality, my mom did a superb job of parenting me. She was firm, but she gave me a long rope, allowing me to hang myself and thus learn from my mistakes. She never berated me for the foolish things I did. When my acts were over and done with, they were truly over and done with, and we moved forward from that point.

My mom's example is now an integral part of the person I am today. This makes the separation from her not painful but sweet. I have not lost my mom, because I know exactly where she is. She has preceded me to heaven and is waiting expectantly for the day I will arrive.

LEAVING A LEGACY

I don't believe there is a mom living who wants her children to grow up remembering her examples of criticism, harshness or rage. If any of these traits are part of the way you mother your children, today can be the beginning of a brand-new legacy of example.

- Apologize to your children when you show negative behaviors, and tell them you desire to change.

- Ask God to remind you whenever you revert to old behaviors.
- Begin right now to be the example you want your children to emulate.

CHAPTER FOUR

The Legacy of Giving

Children are born needing a lot of our time and energy. We give up our rest, our resources and our time—all day, every day—for the sake of our children. The legacy of giving, however, is something more intrinsic than physically giving to our children. The legacy of giving involves much more than our time; it involves the total commitment of our being. Giving is more about our attitude than the actual deeds we do. Giving out of love, not duty, is what I believe creates this legacy.

Life was fairly simple when I grew up in the 1940s and 1950s. Gender roles were more clearly drawn then—the husband worked to bring home money to pay the bills and the wife stayed home to bear and raise the children. Most families only had one car, so life was pretty much centered on the home. With no television or air conditioning, children played outside all day when the weather was good, only coming inside for meals. Day-care centers were few and far between, and most of the women who worked had service jobs such as teaching or nursing so that they could be home when their children were home. Even when I was a teenager, most of my girlfriends had moms who stayed at home during the day.

Life today is radically different. Divorce is the reality for half of all marriages, Christian or not. Many mothers are divorced and raising their children alone or they have never been married, so working outside the home is a necessity, not an option. And let's not forget dads. In today's society, it is not a rarity at all for children to be raised by their dad, while their mom lives apart from her children.

Working outside the home can be an economic necessity for moms; at times, moms work simply because they like to work, and the money helps provide extras such as Christian school tuition, sports activities, dance lessons or music lessons. Whether a mom works outside the home or not, every mom is a working mom.

I stayed home until my youngest child started school, and there was never a dull moment. I was *always* busy. I have the utmost admiration both for stay-at-home moms and for those who juggle full-time motherhood with a job outside the home. It is my personal belief that if a mom needs to work and if she asks for God's direction, He will not only provide for her but for her children as well.

Both of my daughters and my daughter-in-law have been stay-at-home moms who have worked part-time around their children's schedules. My decision to start working was predicated on the need for tuition for the Christian school my children attended. God provided me a job from 8:00 A.M. to 3:00 P.M. at the church where my children went to school, so I was able to be home with them after school.

Even though my mom never worked outside the home and, for the most part, my daughters did not work outside the home, I am a mom who has worked outside the home for many years. I've heard debates on the merits of staying home versus working, and it is easy to take the side of the stay-at-home moms. Surely, we say, staying at home must be better than being gone all day. The reality, I believe, is that having a mom who is always there for her children means much more than just having a mom who is at home. Many moms who stay home are not there for their children at all, and many moms who work outside the home are always there for their children. The reverse is also true.

The secret of the legacy of giving is having a mom who is emotionally there for her children seven days a week, 24 hours a day. Moms who work outside the home and who also want their children to be their highest priority will need to sacrifice some things they would like to do in order to be there for their children. But it is entirely possible to do so. Even though I have always worked, I have never missed a ball game, a birthday or a holiday celebration with my children. My husband and children are my top priorities and my greatest joys in life.

My dear friend Jaye Martin is the mom of one daughter, Kelly. Jaye was trained as an interior designer when God called her into full-time ministry in 1984. She sold her interior-design business and started seminary. About halfway through seminary, much to her surprise, Jaye became pregnant with Kelly. Kelly is now 16 and one of the most well-adjusted teens I have ever known. Jaye has always worked, but Kelly has had 100 percent of her mom from the first day of her life. Jaye has consistently put the needs of her family above the needs of her job as director of women's evangelism at a missions board, and I have watched as her daughter has blossomed into a godly young woman. For the past five years, God has provided the perfect job for Jaye, which has allowed her to work from home during Kelly's extremely important teen years.

Whether we need to work or whether God calls us into His work, He will always provide for our families if we trust Him to make a way.

I learned the legacy of giving by observing my mom's life. She would have been shocked if she heard it said that she was a giving person. Because her giving came from her heart, it was just second nature for her to do the things she did, not only for me, but for many others as well.

I watched as my dad battled congestive heart failure for five years before his death. My mom was brave and courageous as she walked through that time with him. Johnny and I were awakened many times in the middle of the night to call an ambulance for my dad. I was with Mom at the hospital most of the last five weeks of my dad's life. The morning my dad died, I watched as she comforted the hospital chaplain instead of expecting comfort from him.

The actions that represented my mom's heart were always actions that pointed outward. And she didn't think about what she would receive in return. I must have caught that legacy and passed it on to my own two daughters, because giving is such a natural part of their lives.

My daughter Lisa is one of the most giving women I know. You simply cannot outgive Lisa. She wants to have every family party and holiday celebration at her home, and she never cares about how much work this will mean for her. Lisa works outside the home now, but her giving hasn't stopped just because her time is limited. She took a week away from work to be available to cook for our First Place F.O.C.U.S. Week this year. I only have to hint that I need her to help me and she is there in a flash. When she comes to the Bay, she always makes sure that our house is as clean when she leaves as it was when she got there. One Saturday she got up and single-handedly washed every window at our home just because they needed washing and she was there.

And then there's Shari. After Shari's death, her sister-in-law, Yvonne, nominated Shari for the Ruth Award at the 2002 Inspire Conference held at our church in Houston. We were all there the day the award was presented posthumously. Here is a portion of the letter Yvonne wrote. It spells out so beautifully what the legacy of giving means.

> Seven years ago, God orchestrated the events in my life in such a way that everything important to me crumbled all at once. They crumbled and then I crumbled. I had no idea what was happening to me. I cried every day, all day, for months. I went to bed crying, and as soon as I opened my eyes in the morning, the tears poured out. I had fallen into the pit, but not

just the pit, the basement of the basement of the basement of the pit. That last basement is as low as one can get and actually still be alive. I had lost my purpose. I had lost my hope. I had lost my desire to live. I wanted to die.

Shari saw what had happened to me, and she began calling me. For 12 years prior, I had known her only as my sister-in-law, and until that point we hadn't shared much about our personal lives. But that changed very quickly. Every day Shari called me. She listened to me through my tears and encouraged me. We would talk for hours, and each time I hung up the phone, I found myself wondering, *Who is this person?* I had never seen this Shari before. I was baffled at her compassion and generosity toward me. I couldn't figure out why she was helping me, but I didn't question her motivation for very long. I was so desperate that I reached out at anything she offered.

Over the next weeks and months, Shari became my rock. She was the life preserver that kept me from going under. I counted on her phone calls and encouragement. She told me about God and how much He loved me. She told me of His promises and how they were meant for me. As a baby Christian, I listened to her words with both hopeful curiosity and skepticism. I wanted to believe, but I couldn't understand how a God who loved me so much could let me feel so much pain. Shari promised me that all of my pain, confusion and tears served a purpose and that one day, God would make use of everything I was going through.

Sometimes I told her that I didn't know how to believe, and she would say, "Then I will believe for you." At those times, it was her faith that saw both of us through. Shari walked by my side, matching her steps to mine. When I got tired, she let me lean on her; and when I couldn't take another step, God gave her the strength to carry me. When I wanted to give up, she refused to give up on me. She saw value in me that I wasn't able to see, and she was determined to rid me of my blinders. Sometimes I wonder why she came to my rescue. She didn't have to. It was her choice to make. But I'm sure I know the answer: God asked her to do it, and she did what He asked.

It wasn't until several years later that I truly understood the sacrifices Shari had made for me. We were talking about those early days, and I said something that made it apparent to her that I couldn't see the progress I had made. Two sentences put it all in perspective for me. Shari said, "Yvonne, don't you remember how bad it was? It was so bad that I didn't know if I was going to make it through!" I had no idea it had been hard on her because she didn't let me see her struggle. Everything she did for me seemed to be so effortless.

I imagine now the task that stood before Shari. She was looking at me, a woman broken, hurting and bleeding, who had given up on life. She took the challenge God had put before her and said, "Yes, I will try to help Yvonne find her hope. I will try to help her believe in things she doesn't believe exist. I will try to help her choose life over death. With Your help, I will try." That takes true courage and sacrifice. Shari put herself aside and committed to things she wasn't even sure she had the strength to do. She persevered on my behalf, set aside her own fears and trusted in

God to see us through. That's the kind of woman I aspire to be.

The simple truth of it all: Had Shari said no to God's request, chances are that I would be dead—if not physically dead, then emotionally dead. Death was the option I was reaching for. It was the only option I could see until Shari stepped in. Her obedience to God and her personal sacrifice helped me find life. Sounds a little bit like Jesus, doesn't it?

Cara's writing about her mom reveals the things that are truly important to our children. Cara wrote so much on this particular day that I will include the first part of that day here and the last part in the next chapter.

Cara Symank

November 6, 2002

I loved Mom, and I miss her. I miss her laugh. I miss the way she said, "Girls," to my friends and me. It was usually followed by her laughing, looking down toward the floor and then with a smirk looking back up at one of us and saying, "What?" when one of us made another smart comment or just another dumb phrase.

The funny thing about Mom was that she would never make breakfast unless I had friends over or if it was Easter or Christmas morning. That was Mom. She was so goofy. She loved me to death, but she never lacked the ability to make fun of my friends and me. We always wanted her "pigs in a blanket thingies" for breakfast—and they were usually there. On holidays she would stick around for the girls and me to open everything she and Dad had given us, and then she would unnoticeably fade away to the kitchen to make Easter breakfast or Christmas breakfast.

I'm not looking forward to Thanksgiving this year. I wish we could leave from Thanksgiving dinner laughing, like all the other years before—all the others except last year. She made things so fun just because she couldn't go without laughing—well, except for when she was wearing one of her long cotton nightgowns, gritting her teeth at me for something or another. That was Mom, too. She loved nothing more than to sit there on the couch or the chair and read her Bible. The thing is, I know she never did it just so that the girls and I would see her do it. She did it because she wanted to. Back to the gritting of the teeth. It was usually followed by, "Cara, I just don't know. I just don't know." Then she would walk away. Mom never stayed upset for long before she'd come find me again to say she was sorry.

Our daughters catch the legacy of giving during what might seem like inconsequential moments—a brief time of banter and conversation with their friends, the way we make a meal special for them, how quick we are to say we're sorry because we would rather restore the flow of relationship than be right.

The legacy of giving must come from the heart if it is to live on into future generations. Children have an uncanny way of knowing whether we are just doing something because we need to do it or whether we are doing it because we genuinely want to.

So many moms who are overworked and stressed to the max equate giving with purchasing. These moms are constantly buying things for their daughters instead of giving of themselves. Money has nothing to do with the legacy of giving. Giving has to do with sacrifice and having our priorities in the right order.

LEAVING A LEGACY

Prioritizing life is not easy, but it is possible, if you really want to leave a giving legacy. Here are some ideas to help you:

- Turn off the television and have a family night.
- If you work outside the home, take a vacation day and do something special with your daughter.
- Invite your daughter to take a walk with you after dinner this evening. Maybe you'll decide to do it *every* evening!

CHAPTER FIVE

The Legacy of Time

The legacy of giving results from our attitudes about spending time with our daughters; the *legacy of time* is passed on by the actual time we spend with them. For a daughter, nothing takes the place of time spent with Mom.

There is a great deal of talk today about choosing *quality* time over *quantity* time. Moms are so busy that some of them actually make appointments to be with their daughters. I wish it were this easy to leave the legacy of time; but it has been my own experience that I can never schedule quality time; it happens in the most unexpected situations and places, and very seldom is it willed into being with an appointment.

Some of the best times with my daughters took place in the car while I was driving and the two girls were in the backseat. Because I wasn't sitting there looking at them, they said all kinds of things they wouldn't have said otherwise. Just by driving and listening, I found out how life was going for them.

Quality time doesn't end when our daughters are grown. Just recently, my daughter Lisa and I were in the car coming back from the mall. Lisa shared some things with me that were bothering her. Had we not had time alone together, that talk would not have taken place. Every daughter longs for time alone with her mother—time just to talk, to dream, to learn how to become a woman.

I have no memory of a time when my mom wasn't available to me. When I was a child, she was the room mother in my class. She was my Brownie and Girl Scout leader. She went to church camp as a sponsor. She was the director of my Sunday School department when I was a teenager and attended most of the church parties.

My mom was a great seamstress, and if I had a party to attend on Friday night, it was nothing for her to make me a new dress on Friday while I was at school so that I had something new to wear to the party.

When I had a prom coming up, we would go to the most expensive store in town and I would try on the most beautiful dresses in the store. Mom would sit in the dressing room with a pad and pencil. After I picked the dress I wanted, she made notes about the dress and then went home and made the dress for me. I took that gift for granted until I was grown and realized that not all girls, including my own, had a mother like mine.

Even when I had children of my own, my mother sewed all the rips and tears in our clothes and did a lot of sewing for her grandchildren. Every year she made the girls winter coats—one for Lisa, one for Shari and one for my niece, Julie. I remember that one year, when Barbie dolls first made their debut, my mom made wardrobes for the girls' three Barbie dolls, complete with bridal dresses and winter coats, identical to the coats she had made for each girl.

I am amazed at how much my daughter Shari was like my mom. Shari learned to sew at an early age because she demanded that my mom teach her. One summer, when Mom had all six grandchildren at her home on Galveston Bay, Shari persisted in her request until Mom taught her to sew. Shari then made several halter tops for herself, her sister and her cousin. Mom spent her time running to the store to get more material for Shari's sewing projects!

When Shari had three girls of her own, she made them beautiful smocked dresses. I've heard that talent skips a generation. There must be something to that, because the talent to sew certainly skipped right over me.

As a teenager, when I came in from a date, Mom always got out of bed, even if she had been asleep, and sat on the other twin bed in my room while I got ready for bed. She always wanted to know how the evening had gone and was genuinely interested in everything that had transpired. Sometimes I was happy when I came home, and sometimes I was upset. Mom was always there to make it better when things were not going well.

I never remember thinking my mom had gotten up to spy on me or check up on me, although, looking back, that's not a bad idea for parents to do. I didn't know that not all moms did that sort of thing, because it seemed so natural to me. The legacy continued with my children, because they always came in and woke us up when they came home from a date. I regret that I didn't get up each and every time they came home, because those times would be precious memories for me today.

My mom was definitely a hands-on parent, and her availability did not stop when I was grown. Mom was there for me at the birth of each of my three children, and she was always available to help. When Johnny and I married, I had just graduated from high school, and Johnny was in his second year of college. Our daughter Lisa was born during the 14 months we lived with my parents after we married.

I had toxemia during that pregnancy and was very sick after Lisa's birth. I vividly remember how my mom cared for all of us during those first weeks of Lisa's life.

Lisa was born in the month of January. Every morning, Mom took a pillow into the bathroom, turned on the heater and gave Lisa her bath while I watched. One month after Lisa was born, Mom looked at me and said, "Tomorrow, she's all yours. You're going to love giving this baby her baths."

Mom was gentle and kind, but she knew that I had watched long enough and needed to take over the job of being a full-time mom to my child. I remember that precious time, and now, having children and grandchildren of my own, I know the concern my mom must have had for me. I was 18 years old with a baby of my own. I had never done much babysitting as a teenager, so I learned from my mom how to be a mom during those first months of Lisa's life.

Mom took all six of her grandkids to the Bay for a week at a time during summer. Later in life, when I expressed amazement at this, her only comment was, "Now, which one could I have left home?"

Mom was always glad to babysit my three children, but I learned to always have a backup plan in the event something fun came up for her and my dad to do. It was not unusual for her to call and say, "Some friends have invited us to dinner. Do you think you can find someone else to keep the kids?" Mom was available, but her life did not revolve around my life. The fact that she had a life of her own was a great blessing after my dad died in 1976, because she had so many friends who still wanted to include her in their plans. Mom had a healthy view of being a mother, and she had the wonderful attribute of being available without keeping a stranglehold on her two daughters.

I carried on that legacy by being available to stay a week with my daughters each time they had their own babies. Those times are some of the sweetest memories in my memory bank—cleaning house and doing laundry so that my daughters were free to recover and love on their babies. Lisa and Shari had two of their children just 11 days apart, so I stayed with Shari for a week when Christen was born, and after just a few days at home, I went for another week when Lisa gave birth to Katherine. Twenty-four years earlier, my sister, Glenda, and I gave birth to her Julie and my Shari just 10 days apart. Shari and Julie grew up just like sisters, and I knew the same would be true for Christen and Katherine.

All of us lead busy lives, and most daughters will not share their innermost thoughts and concerns just because Mom has made an appointment with her for lunch or shopping. So let me share more of Cara's

November 6, 2002, journal entry, which comes from the heart of a young woman who no longer has time available with her mom.

Cara Symank

[My mom] was the poster mom of up close and personal. If I came home from school upset and she had the slightest indication that I was upstairs crying, she would come upstairs and walk into my extremely unwelcoming room. If she didn't come soon enough, I would let out a few louder screeches or make sure to sigh, or I would take a big gasp in the middle of uncontrollable tears—that one always got her moving. She would sit beside me and ask what was wrong. I always wanted her there, yet I didn't want to tell her what was going on. She never forgot those key things that I wish I hadn't said. She only wanted me to tell her so that she could stop me from hurting the next time or so that she could simply fix it. I wish I could have seen that from the very beginning.

She was the kind of mom who wanted me to deal with all of my emotions. She couldn't understand my lack of dealing with my emotions. She would have much rather seen me sit on the couch with her and talk about what was bothering me deep down rather than see me go out to the basketball game. She would give me that half smile and say, "Sue." My friends reminded me over and over of the way my mom called me Sue. She didn't just call me Sue—she would say it as a sigh. It was what she said when she had nothing more to say.

It was what she said when she really just wanted Rachel and me to go to bed and be quiet. It was what she said when Jana and I just couldn't contain the urge to talk about some of the other high school girls in a mean way. It was what she said when she wanted me to go all the way downstairs (while she was sitting on the couch downstairs, I might mention) to get her coffee from the kitchen, with the cream *and* the sugar. And she would have to tell me every time from the other room how to do it. I would inevitably ask, "Is it two spoons of sugar and one spoon of cream or one spoon of sugar and two spoons of cream?" I know that she also secretly got a thrill out of sending me to the grocery store. It would have been much simpler to do it herself. I think she put things on that list that she knew I'd mess up on. I swear she did. She gave me heck for it, but I know she enjoyed it at the same time.

I was her baby. She always talked about when she had me she didn't think she could ever love anything so much. Oh, she had her traits that clashed with mine! She was so . . . hmm . . . outspoken about how she really felt. The phrase I would hear more than anything is, "You need to be more assertive!" She always waited until I was done crying about what someone had done to me, and then it would come. It was just what I could expect to be said. My dad understands. She said it to him *all the time* (and he didn't have to be crying; she just periodically informed him when she was irritated that someone had walked all over him and he wasn't even doing anything to change it). That was Mom. I didn't always understand her, but I'm starting to understand her a lot better.

Nothing in the world was more important to her than my dad and her girls. Her entire life was devoted to the four of us. I think her life was devoted to her three girls long before any of us ever existed. She would always talk about how she was 15 when she knew my dad was the one, and she had dreamed up the girls and me long before she ever saw my dad (although, I'm not quite sure we are exactly what she dreamed up).

She loved us even more in real life than she thought she would when she believed that we would be perfect. Mom loved us. In fact, her very dying words were "Tell the girls I love them." I saw it. I saw her sit up one last time to say something to my dad. And one more time I saw my dad lean in toward her to hear what it was that she was saying. When I saw her sit up in the front yard that night, and I saw him step toward her and lean down, I also saw a look of calm on my dad's face. I bet it was on her face, too, although I could only see the back of her head. He just seemed to be listening to her say something, as he would have any other day. It was right after that moment that everything in my life changed.

I've recently begun to tell my dad that I just want things to be normal again. But I guess I can't do anything about the fact that I will never have her back. I wish she would show up this Christmas morning in her cotton gown with multiple holes in it so that she could sit there with her coffee cup and slurp occasionally. Life was fun—not always great, but fun. I miss her. As much as I've suppressed a lot of these thoughts until now, I promise not to forget anymore. I want to remember.

LEAVING A LEGACY

Life goes by so fast, and some of us never seem to make time for those who are most important to us. Days, weeks and even months can go by without spending any quality time together. If you want to do a better job of leaving a legacy of time, here are some suggestions:

- Ask God to show you the areas where you waste precious time that could be given to your family.
- Think about what you would do with your daughter today if you knew you would not have her tomorrow.
- Do today whatever just came to mind.

CHAPTER SIX

The Legacy of Character

Much, if not most, of the character qualities I possess today is a result of what my mom and dad modeled. They learned to appreciate what really counts in life. One of those qualities was care for others.

When I was about 10, my mom asked me to befriend a girl at Sunday School. She said, "Suzanne doesn't have many friends. Why don't you ask her to sit with you in church?" I was glad to do that, and before long, Suzanne invited me over to her house after church on Sunday afternoon. We became the best of friends and spent many hours together from that time through the end of high school.

My mom was always volunteering to help someone in need. I took these things for granted, but the legacy that was passed on to me has been passed on to my children. It's so true that children do what we do, not what we say.

My mom was always giving someone a ride to church. It was a normal occurrence for us to stop at several houses on Wednesday afternoon on the way to Wednesday-night church services. Because most families only had one car, Mom picked up the ladies, and their husbands came to church from work.

After I was grown, my mom taught ESL (English as a Second Language) classes for many years. She usually taught English to Japanese women. Each of them became her very good friend.

My mom and dad brought my dad's parents to Houston to live while my own children were young. Mom regularly took them to the store and to doctor's appointments. I never heard her complain that these were my dad's parents, not hers, or that it wasn't fair. My dad had severe heart disease and was hospitalized many times during this period of caring for his parents, so Mom did the lion's share of work.

Children know instinctively what is most important to their parents. As a child reared in a middle-class home, I never knew what it meant to do without, but I also never knew what it meant to be rich in material wealth. Material possessions had little relevance to my mother. I remember moving to a new home when I was 12 years old. My parents rented out our old house for a few years, and even though our new house was much nicer and bigger, I remember Mom saying many times, "It wouldn't bother me one bit if we had to move back to our old house."

After Dad died, Mom sold their home and bought a condominium right next door to our church. Because the condo was much smaller than their home, Mom didn't have room for much of the furniture. Yet

I never got the impression that she was the least bit grieved to sell furniture and possessions. Her attitude was that these things had served her well when they were needed, but they were just things, and things are replaceable.

When I celebrated my fortieth birthday, my mom started giving me family heirlooms for birthday presents. She wanted me to enjoy those things while she was still alive. A few years before Mom died, she started giving her grandchildren family heirlooms with a little note tucked inside each one to explain where the item came from and to whom it had originally belonged. When the time came for Mom to move in with me, she never complained about having to leave her possessions behind. The legacy of character Mom passed on to me was that the only real happiness is found in people, not in possessing things. She believed that if the people we love are with us, we are rich indeed.

Because my mom lived out her view on material possessions, I have never been tied to things. This legacy was extremely valuable when my own family went through a fire in 1974 and we had to leave our home for three months. Everything in our attic had been destroyed, and some of the things lost had great sentimental value. I had saved all of the beautiful formals my mom had made when I was in high school. My hope had been that my own daughters would wear them and enjoy the legacy Mom had passed on to them through me.

All of our Christmas decorations stored in the attic were destroyed in the fire. Our children were 14, 12 and 10 at the time of the fire, so I had kept and treasured many ornaments they had made over the years. I'll never forget my mom and dad coming into the house after the fire. Our neighbors and friends were all there, and we were laughing and talking. When my mom walked through the door and saw us, she burst into tears and said, "I don't know how you can be laughing at a time like this!" What she didn't realize was that I had learned from her that the things we had lost were just stuff, and stuff could be replaced.

When our son's home burned in 1997, his family lost literally everything they owned. A year and a half later, when they moved into their rebuilt home, I was amazed that they had already replaced all their stuff again. In other words, they were able to move beyond what was lost. They had received the legacy passed on from Mom that people are priceless; possessions are not.

We are blessed to have our wonderful home on Galveston Bay. There will come a day when we will not have this home any longer, but Johnny and I will always have the memories of the time we spent there together and the time we spent there with our family and friends. Jesus tells us to store up treasures in heaven, not on Earth (see Matt. 6:19-20). My mom passed on a precious legacy of character to me by not being tied to her possessions.

When my mom could no longer care for herself, it was a very natural thing for me to care for her in my home. I counted it a great privilege to be able to repay, in a small way, what she had done for others and for me.

I'm sure that I love people so much today because of my mom's legacy of loving others. Many times we don't think about the character qualities our mothers possessed until they are no longer living. Cara wrote about Shari's character and what it means in her life today. No doubt, what Shari expressed by her life was passed down from my mom through me and will live on in all the generations of our family to follow.

Cara Symank

A Mother's Character

I completely understand what you're going through. I know it is very difficult and discouraging at times. As hard as it may be to do, try and remember who is really in charge: the One who has ultimate authority and who certainly is in control. When we focus on our circumstances instead of on our Christ, things start to get cloudy and distorted. I want to encourage you to keep your eyes on Christ. He will make you okay even in a situation that seems everything but okay. I can testify to that. Go back and recount what He's already done for you. He is faithful to complete what He started.

SHARI ANNE SYMANK, WRITTEN IN A CARD TO HER
SISTER-IN-LAW, YVONNE

It is now a year after my mom's death, and my mind and heart are only beginning to comprehend the magnitude of who my mother was and who she remains to be as reflected through my two younger sisters and me. Her level of compassion for people was so intense that most individuals were unable to grasp it. Her heart and every emotion were dedicated to the needs of others.

After living an entire year without her compassionate love for me, I have begun to understand exactly what it is that I am now lacking. It has only been recently, as I am approaching adulthood, that I begin to understand that my mother's character was not average, that not everyone is fortunate enough to receive the genuine kind of love that my sisters and I received.

A short time after losing my mother, I discovered that she had kept a journal. In recent months, I have seen the journal on a few occasions and have had the desire to read a page or two. I had never read enough to grasp the purpose of the journal. One day, as I quietly sat reflecting my own thoughts onto paper, I had the urgent desire to know the inner thoughts my mother had on things. Not more than a minute had passed before I phoned my father for permission to go home and get the journal.

As I opened the colorfully printed journal, I immediately was able to rekindle the part of my mother's personality that so wanted everything to be full of life and colorful. As I read, it soon became apparent that her purpose for writing was to capture some of her prayers and some of the things that God was revealing to her. I embraced the joy of being able to read over these truths because it quickly reminded me of the numerous times she would talk to me about God on hour-long drives into Houston. She was never one to keep to herself her beliefs about the power of God.

As I continued to read, I felt the desire to know her thoughts about daily life. I was amazed to find that she felt like God was telling her to write about everything, rather than only the spiritual side of herself. Yet she battled that idea and continued to write very little about daily activities, explaining that she did not understand why she was being asked to write about everything. One entry read:

> Writing a spiritual journal is fine, but that's only one part of me. What about the day-to-day stuff? What are we doing? How are we spending our time? I think God wants me to see that He created all the sides of who I am, not just the spiritual. I still don't understand why it takes me so long sometimes to understand what He's trying to say to me. I wish it were easier. But I know if it were, it wouldn't require much faith.

We seem to always want a reason for the tasks God calls us to do, yet the sovereignty of God is such that we may never know the entirety of why He calls us to do specific things. We must simply listen without questioning His ultimate purpose. Several times my mom quoted Jeremiah 29:11 in her journal, as she was having trouble grasping the *whys* of her callings. May we all remind ourselves that God has a plan for each of us.

Of her entries, the one most intriguing to me was written in March 1997:

> I think it is so interesting how the first words recorded that God spoke were, "Let there be light," in Genesis 1:3. In Matthew 5:14 Jesus said, "You are the light of the world. A city on a hill cannot be hidden." We are the only true light the world will ever see amidst all the darkness. I think the point is for us to see that even we alone make such a difference depending on how we live life. We never know how it may affect another life. Our light, if shining openly, might cause a spark in another life. This is an important lesson to remember when I start doubting and wondering how I can really make a difference in this great big world.

After reading that particular entry, I was able to rejoice. Despite my sorrow in the loss of my mother, I knew that she desired to be used by God, and through her death He was certainly able to use her life as a testimony. On the very night her life was taken, both my father's brother and mother accepted Jesus Christ as their personal Lord and Savior. They were able to reflect upon my mother's life and were reminded of the many times that she endeavored to talk about God at the dinner table, desiring to have every single one of her family members become believers in the God who was so real and amazing to her.

Character is an elusive quality; it is hard to nail down. All Christians should be people of character, but we all know professing Christians who lack character in many areas. If we, as mothers, fail to exhibit strength of character in what we do and say, then our daughters will likely model the weaknesses in our behavior when they are grown.

In December 1984, I finally sold out totally to the Lordship of Jesus Christ in my life. During the next six years, God was faithful to cleanse me of patterns of sin that still resided in me. I certainly don't want to imply that I live a life of sinless perfection today—anyone who knows me knows that isn't true. My reason for writing about the monumental changes in me since 1984 is to say that there is sin still present in my life today that I call character flaws—characteristics such as pride, the tendency to gossip, rudeness and thoughtlessness—which I don't want to pass on to future generations. When I began praying a number of years ago that God would make me into a godly woman, I didn't have a clue what the answer to that prayer might entail. I continue to pray the same prayer today, because I want to leave a godly legacy of character to my family that will honor God when I am gone.

LEAVING A LEGACY

If you didn't receive a legacy of character from your mother, then you must learn how to do the right thing, for the sake of your children. One basic character trait is honesty. This means something as seemingly small as telling the clerk when you have received too much change or when one of the items in the checkout basket is left off the bill. You may need to work hard at not giving in to consumerism hype and shopping-mall mania, or else risk leaving a legacy of materialism to your children.

Our daughters are watching us to see if we have character or if we just profess to have it. Let me leave you with a few character-building suggestions:

- Ask God to point out the character flaws He sees in you.
- Look for ways to model character every day. (Hint: These are often the little things we think are inconsequential but are actually cumulative in effect.)
- Praise your daughter when she exhibits strength of character.

CHAPTER SEVEN

The Legacy of Words

One of the things I loved most about my mom was her quick wit and her way with words. Mom didn't spend hours lecturing about any subject; she just threw out the advice and you could take it or not. Many times, after I was grown with children of my own, she would say to me, "Now I know you are going to do what you want, but I just have to say this . . ." She would then give the advice—end of subject.

I heard my friend Kay tell someone the other day, "When Carole's mom died, Carole lost her biggest cheerleader." Kay went on to tell a story of being on a business trip with me in Tennessee. Mom and another good friend, Joy Stephens, joined us for part of the trip. We took them to a trout farm. This was a fun place, because you caught your own fish, watched it being cleaned and then took it into the restaurant to be prepared. The pond was well stocked, and the water was so clear that we could see fish swimming everywhere. Well, I was the only one of the group who couldn't seem to catch a fish.

My mom kept telling everyone that there must be something wrong with the hook or I would already have caught a fish! I always took for granted that my mom would stand up for me, but I now know that many children live with constant criticism from a mom or dad who should be their greatest cheerleader. By having a mom who always cheered me on, I can see that God is doing the same thing for me—He cheers me on every day. Moms who are cheerleaders for their daughters pass on what is probably the most valuable legacy of all.

Since Mom's death, so many of her wise and witty sayings have come back to me. I want to share with you some of those sayings and what I learned from them.

ON MARRIAGE

Don't do anything outside the perimeter of the house, unless you want to.

Johnny and I lived with my mom and dad for the first 14 months after we married. They were busy building a house on Galveston Bay, and they gave us their master bedroom and bath. They were smart enough to know that with Johnny in college and working part-time for my dad, we would never be able to buy a house unless they helped us. I didn't know it at the time, but my dad encouraged Johnny to buy savings bonds each pay period. At the end of the first year, Johnny surprised me with enough money to make the down payment on our first home. Believe it or not, our first home had three bedrooms, one bath and a one-car garage for the selling price of $10,700, with payments of $72 per month. (Of course, when you only brought home $116 per week, $72 was quite a bit to pay each month!)

When we moved into the house, Mom laughingly said, "Don't do anything outside the perimeter of the house, unless you want to." She went on to say that whatever a wife starts doing, such as yard work, taking out the trash, plumbing or painting, she will have to keep doing. I didn't think much about her words at the time, but I have watched them proved to be true time and again. I have friends whose husbands don't mow the lawn as quickly as the wife wants, and when the men do mow the grass, it doesn't meet with the wife's approval. Before long, the wife begins mowing the yard and it becomes her permanent job. Every time I help Johnny in the yard (by riding the lawn mower), I chuckle inside as I think about my mom's words.

I have more than one friend who takes out the trash twice a week because her husband doesn't get it out soon enough, or he forgot to take it out a few times, so she took over the job. There were times in our early years of marriage that the trash didn't get taken out on Tuesday, and I found that if I didn't run it out to the street, Johnny managed to get it all out by Friday, without my saying a word. I believe Mom had the wisdom to know that wives can easily emasculate their husbands by constantly nagging or by taking on every job around the house. When the husband doesn't feel needed, he stops trying.

I broke your plate.

When we bought our first home, I spent weeks getting everything moved from my mom and dad's house to the new home. I was such a mama's girl that I couldn't seem to move the last important item, Lisa's baby bed. You see, if I didn't move Lisa's bed, then we hadn't really moved yet. One day, I came back to Mom's from a day of playing house in our new home to find Lisa's baby bed disassembled and in the garage. When I asked Mom why she had taken Lisa's bed down, she said, "I had to break your plate." She then went on to explain to me that in the old days, when a child left home, the saying was, "I broke your plate." That simply meant that you no longer had a place to eat at the family table, so you had to make it on your own. My feelings were hurt a little, but Johnny and I moved the bed that evening and spent that night in our new home. My wise mom knew that without a little nudge from her, I would drag out forever what I thought would be a painful separation.

Why buy the cow if you can get the milk for free?

Mom was way ahead of her time on this one. Very few people lived together outside of marriage during the years when I grew up. Mom used this statement regarding girls having sex before marriage. This wouldn't be a bad saying for girls to hear today as they consider living with a guy before marriage.

ON GIVING ADVICE

Everyone pays her own ticket.

I have a long history of driving too fast and have taken defensive-driving classes more than once to keep a speeding ticket from appearing on my permanent driving record. For years, if I was driving my mom's car too fast, Mom would say those words to tell me that I needed to slow down a bit. If I chose not to, then the ticket would be mine to pay. This must have been her adaptation of "You reap what you sow."

I don't know if this is a problem or not, but . . .

My mom said this when she thought something was a problem and wanted to let me know about it. One day, when Lisa was three, Mom drove up to our house, got out of the car, came inside and said, "I don't know if this is a problem or not, but Lisa is in the top of the pine tree in your backyard." Lisa had been climbing trees since the first time she went outside to play. The first time she climbed a tree, she was barely two, and Johnny ran inside to get a camera before he got her out of the tree. I assured Mom that Lisa would be fine, because she was sure-footed, and Mom let it go at that! Looking back, what three-year-old is fine at the top of a 35-foot pine tree, accompanied by the little four-year-old boy from next door?!

ON WORRY

The things we worry about never happen.

My mom was not a worrier, and her mom was not a worrier, so this was one of Mom's favorite sayings when someone talked about worrying. For the most part, this is a true saying, because people rarely think about worrying about the bizarre things that actually happen to them. One of my granddaughters, who *is* a worrier, said that if the things we worry about never happen, then that's a good reason to worry. Kids are smarter today than I was—I accepted Mom's saying at face value. The truth is, worry is one of those things that is caught by children more than it is taught to them. If your mom was a worrier, you caught the habit, and it's a hard one to break.

My mom left me a precious legacy. By watching her consistent faith that God would provide, and then seeing Him actually do it, I can say that I live worry free.

This too shall pass.

I heard this wise counsel from Mom on many occasions as she talked to women about the problems they were having either in their marriages or with one of their children. The best part of being a Christian who perseveres through trouble is that God plans for us to learn more through suffering than through good times. I wish that I would learn during times of prosperity and ease, but those are the times I tend to coast. Invariably, it is during the really rough times that my roots go down deep with God, and later—usually much later—I can see everything that God taught me during a particular trial.

ON DIETING

If jelly beans were alcohol, I'd be drunk
every time I got home from
the grocery store.

My mom absolutely loved jelly beans. When she went to the grocery store, she always bought a bag of jelly beans, which hung on a rack by the checkout counter, and then proceeded to eat every one of them before she got home.

I had to finally learn that I simply
could not eat up every good
thing on this earth.

Mom was saying that we live our lives in a way that suggests that if we don't eat something right now, it will never come around again. What she wanted to teach my sister and me was that good food tends to come around more than once, and if we don't eat something this time, it will surely come around again!

ON OLD AGE

My mind doesn't know my body is getting old.

I heard Mom say this many times, and as I have aged, I know exactly what she meant. Even though I am past 60, it seems like yesterday that I was a young married woman with three little children. How time flies! I think often, and am amazed, that when my dad died my mom was just two years older than I am right now. I thought they were both pretty old at the time!

Old age is not for sissies.

Mom had a note pad with these words engraved on it, and this was one of her mottos as she aged. It seemed that the older Mom became, there was always something going wrong with her physical health. This saying shows how lightly Mom took the hardships that we all will face if we live long enough. I pray that her positive outlook during trials will live on for many years through me and the generations to come.

Cara shares how words don't always have to be sweet if they are spoken in love. A daughter usually understands why her mom is distressed, so words spoken during those times don't change the fundamental relationship if the relationship is built on love.

Cara Symank

I can remember very few times that my mother did not speak encouraging words to me. I am now certain that there were times that she stretched her imagination as far as it could possibly take her in order to find the positive in the situations I found myself in from time to time. However, there was one time in particular that she simply had no encouraging words to say. This incident occurred the day I announced that I was applying to Texas A&M University and then went on to explain that I only had one day until the application deadline.

I was not the studious type. I was the child who sheepishly arrived at the foot of my parents' bed approximately every six weeks to hand them the dreaded progress report, along with a few tears and the words, "I just do not understand. It is not my fault. I wish I were not dumb, too, you know. You cannot be mad at me for not being smart. Please just sign it so that I can get it turned in. I promise it will not happen next time."

Each time this happened, Mom said she knew better than to think I was incapable of doing better. And each and every time, I pleaded stupidity and explained that it would simply be unreasonable for her to hold that trait against me. This went on for years. It carried me through junior high and all the way through my junior year of high school.

One can see why it may have come as such a shock to my mother when I announced that I was applying to one of the top three universities in the state of Texas. Perhaps it was even more alarming that I had decided to strive for this goal only a week previously, somehow forgetting to discuss my goal with my family. Regardless of the fact that Mom had every reason to doubt my judgment, my mind was made up and I refused to back down. Her lack of encouragement did absolutely nothing to slow me down. I only went on to tell her that if I was going to have everything in on time, I needed to make a trip up to the school with money for the university's application fee. Words cannot describe her facial expressions that day in the kitchen.

"Cara, why do you not think things through?" she said sternly, from across the kitchen. "When are you ever going to settle down? I wish you would sit down and think for just two seconds about what it is that you are saying to me. When did you decide this? I thought you were going to apply later. What are you thinking about? How in the world do you think this is going to work? Do you even have the grades? I do not understand this."

In all fairness to my mom, I must say that as she was speaking those words, she sat down at the kitchen table to write out a check to the university. Without saying anything more, she handed me a check and said, "We will talk about this later." Happy to be on my way out of the kitchen, I quickly set out for my friend's house to tell her that I was set and that the next day we would be able to take everything I needed up to Texas A&M.

As planned, or *far* from planned, rather, my friend Jana and I reached the university only 15 minutes prior to the absolute latest moment that my application would be accepted for review. Jana had not only applied long before the deadline, but she had also graduated at the top of her class. The odds were well against me at this point. Having nothing more than a prayer that I would be accepted, Jana and I laughed all the way home about the lack of planning involved in my decision and how hilarious it would be if I were actually to receive an acceptance letter.

Time went by and I gave very little thought about being anywhere other than at a junior college at home for the spring semester of 2002.

Meanwhile Jana often spoke of being ready to move to College Station. Each and every time she mentioned it, I would say, "I am going to be upset when you are gone."

A short time later, I was faced with my mother's unexpected death on Thanksgiving night. Before she died, my mother's attitude had become the opposite of her attitude when she responded to me that day in the kitchen after I had announced my decision to apply to Texas A&M. In fact, she had grown increasingly excited for me. She asked on a daily basis if I had received anything from the university. On the night of Thanksgiving, as we were walking out to the vehicle, my mother's words to me were "Let's go home so that we can check the Internet to see if you were accepted." Not even three minutes later, an intoxicated driver struck her and left her lifeless body lying in the front yard of my grandparents' house.

The last conversation my mother and I had consisted of her eagerness to know whether I had been accepted to the university of my choice. So it was a somewhat surreal experience when Jana came walking in the front door of my grandmother's home the next afternoon, waving my acceptance letter high in the air. I cried uncontrollably as my aunt and Jana held me. I immediately called my father, who was on his way to the funeral home. He calmly said how proud he was of me. Less than five minutes later, he called me back, tearfully affirming that he had understood me correctly and congratulating me once again.

Oh, the power of words! They can soothe or hurt, heal or scar. A mother's words to her daughter are never forgotten. Wounded women I have spoken with often tell me they still hear their mothers' harsh words playing over in their minds. The saddest part is that sometimes these wounded women say those same hurtful words to their own daughters.

The mind—with a capacity like a supercomputer—stores not only words but also the facial expressions attached to those words. Thanks to all the pop psychology available to moms today, it is not uncommon to hear a mother in a store smiling and saying sweetly to her little girl, "That hurts Mommy when you kick her," or "That hurts Mommy's feelings when you talk like that." What kind of message does that give to a child? There is a disconnection between our words and their intended message when we smile at our misbehaving children for fear their psyches will be damaged. The truth is that we only succeed in confusing our children about our role as parents. God gave us words to use, which needn't be abusive, when we are displeased. He also gave us words to use when we are happy. In my opinion, our society has taken a wrong turn somewhere when it comes to the loving discipline of children.

LEAVING A LEGACY

The legacy of words is probably the most powerful and lasting legacy of all. Words have such power that a mother's words can tear down or build up a daughter's future view of life. Here's what you can do today to change your legacy of words to your daughter:

- Ask God to remind you every time you use words that hurt or have the potential to scar your daughter's view of herself and of the world.
- Use words that bless your daughter. Tell her "I'm so proud of you" or "I'm so glad God gave you to me as my daughter."
- When your daughter needs correction, use words that convey what needs to be done without wounding her spirit.

CHAPTER EIGHT

The Legacy
of Faith

As I stood at the funeral home, I was struck with the sensation of feeling like an orphan. My last link to my earthly parents was now broken. Mom's mind and body had been in a state of decline for the last two years of her life, but as long as she was breathing, I still had her. As I gazed at her body, I thanked God for a mom who had loved Him and had loved me.

I am the woman I am today because of my mom's influence. Every daughter can say the same thing, regardless of whether her mom was a good one or not. It has been said that a mother is the heart of the home. When a mother's heart doesn't know Jesus, the children will lack that vital legacy of faith.

As a five-year-old child in 1947, my life radically changed when my mom and dad became Christians. Our family moved to Houston in 1942 during the height of World War II because my dad needed a job. Jobs were hard to find, but Dad heard that there were jobs in Houston. He went to work at the shipyard while Mom stayed home with my sister, Glenda, and me. My parents were good people who had not yet found Christ.

My sister and I were taken to Sunday School each Sunday by a couple that owned a drugstore in our neighborhood. One Sunday, my sister's choir was singing in church and Dad went to hear her sing. Mom stayed home, because she wasn't feeling well. My dad returned home from church a changed man. He looked the same on the outside, but inside he had changed. He took my mom back to church that same Sunday evening, and my mom accepted Christ at the end of the service. My life is different today because of the simple decision my parents made that particular Sunday to accept Jesus Christ as their Savior.

As a five-year-old, I was old enough to observe the changes in our home. My parents stopped playing poker every Friday night, and we found ourselves attending church socials instead. Mom would say, "We didn't have to drop our old friends. They dropped us like a hot potato when they found out we had become Christians." The change in my parents' lives was genuine, and it lasted until they took their last breath on this earth.

A loving mom is a blessing to her children, but a mom who loves Jesus becomes a legacy of faith to them. "Her children arise and call her blessed" (Prov. 31:28), not because of her inherent goodness, but because of the goodness of God. Shari would agree with that.

Our daughter Shari was shy, and even though she loved to have fun, she never wanted to draw attention to herself. She would be genuinely embarrassed that Cara and I are writing about her, and she'd want to know *why* we were doing it!

SHARI'S LEGACY OF FAITH

I vividly remember Shari accepting Christ at a backyard Bible club when she was seven years old. To my knowledge, she never once doubted her decision.

I saw such spiritual growth in Shari the last few years of her life, and I could see God working in her on a daily basis as she began to study her Bible and spend time alone with Him. Many mornings I arrived at my office to hear a ringing phone. It would be Shari asking a question about her Bible study for that day. She would read the Scripture to me, tell me what her answer was and ask my opinion. I would then tell her what I thought and we would talk it over. The amazing thing about Shari was that she didn't just want to know the answer; she wanted to know the *right* answer, and she studied until she found it. Shari had been like that from the time she was very small, and in that we were quite different. When I do a Bible study, I just want to get the blank filled in so that I can go on to the next question.

Jeff asked Bible teacher Beth Moore to speak at Shari's memorial service. He gave Beth all five of the Beth Moore Bible studies Shari had completed and said, "See if you can find something to use at her service." Beth began her portion of the service with these words:

> When I am inundated by what I do not know, and do not understand, I concentrate on what I *do* know. There are three things I know in this situation. At the top of my list, I know Jesus, and Shari knew Jesus. Believing in God does not carry us in a time of trauma; *knowing* Him does. I know who He is; He is good. I know that Shari's testimony is complete. A faithful life has a continuing effect for a thousand generations. We might think her death is premature, but Revelation 11:7 says, "When they have finished their testimony." Shari marked this planet with her testimony, and it will have ramifications.

Beth said that because Shari was so involved as a wife and mother, our first reaction to her death was, "How will her family make it?" She said, "They will make it because of how involved she was." She looked at the girls and said, "That's how you will make it! Because she invested so much in you—like treasures in a treasure box, like savings for you—that every time you need to, you will draw out of what she has already invested and it will carry you until you see her face-to-face."

I was amazed as Beth went on to share something Shari had written in one of the Bible studies.

Thank You, Lord, that You want to spend time with me each day. That was Your plan. You are enough. He wants me to see that I give my time to Him, not just out of obedience, but because it is a delight and a privilege to do so. Thank You, Lord, for helping me see the difference. It makes me feel special that God actually takes time just for me. It is the intimate time when He reveals Himself to me in a confirming way, maybe just by leading me to a certain Scripture. That is a key factor in what drives me to do His will; kids will do as they see, not as they are told.

I was so proud as I listened and realized how much Shari had poured herself into those studies. I told Beth

later, "If I die, do not look at my studies to find something to say about me. All I do is answer the questions!" Shari's time spent writing in her Bible studies
and in her prayer journal is a huge part of the legacy of
faith she has left for her girls.

Although it took Cara about 18 months before she
was able to look at her momma's prayer journals,
I know that in the years to come, all three of the girls will
go there time and again when they need their momma.

Beth also shared a story about her meeting one of
Amanda's teachers (Amanda is Shari's youngest daughter). The teacher mentioned that after Amanda had been
late for school a number of times, and since Amanda was
such a good student, she asked her, "Amanda, why all the
tardiness?" Amanda replied, "It's my mom. She can't get
out of her Bible for us to get here on time."

After Shari's service a friend of mine came up to
me and said, "I need to make some big changes. I don't
want to die and have my kids remember me sitting
around reading romance novels."

Beth concluded her part of the service by reading
another one of Shari's entries:

In this He has shown me things one by one,
little by little. I believe this is preparing me to

be able to see more of His glory in the future. Lord, You are truly the source of my strength and my ability to do anything. Please give me the courage to continue to pursue You. Lord, I stand in awe of You, of your might and power. You are the only One big enough to take care of our needs. I love You. Thank You, God, that You are all knowing. You truly do work all things for the good for those who love You. Thank You, Lord, that You had it all planned before the foundation of the world.

When Jeff's sister, Yvonne, got up to speak, she talked about how Shari had helped her through a very difficult time in her life. She then focused on the girls and how each had responded to the tragedy. The legacy of faith from their mother is clearly evident in their lives. Yvonne related that Cara had said to her, "I just want to see the purpose in all this. I want to testify to somebody." At the scene of the accident, Cara had walked up to the police car where the young woman who struck Shari was seated, but the girl was too inebriated for Cara to witness to her. About Christen, Yvonne said, "Christen has Christ in her name, her face and her actions. When I think of

Christen, I think of the word 'percolate.' Even though she is the quietest of the three girls, she will be all right, because her thoughts are always percolating." Amanda, who was 13 at the time of the accident, had said to Yvonne and her brother Ronnie, "Thank you for helping us keep our focus." Yvonne's parting words at the memorial service were "I want you to remember Shari; to do that, look at those girls. They are part of those strands in the weaving. Shari has given them something to weave into their lives."

Jeff then came to the platform. He had never spoken in public but did an eloquent job that day. He shared a poem written by Amanda.

Momma
There is a special person
That no one can replace.
Her name is Momma,
And I long to touch her face.

I hear her in my dreams,
I see her in my thoughts.
That special memory of Momma
Will never be forgot.

How could she leave, I wonder?
How could she leave so soon?
She was so young,
Yet her life went with a boom.

The Lord has shown us grace,
A love beyond imagine.
But He will take care of us
Because the Lord was her passion.

My nephew, Rick, led the music for Shari's service and sang "I Can Only Imagine,"[1] a song about what it will be like to be in heaven and how we will react to being in God's presence. At the end of the service, he led us in the old hymn "Blessed Assurance." The beginning words are "Blessed assurance, Jesus is mine; O what a foretaste of glory divine!"[2] Before we sang, Rick looked at my mom and said, "Grandma, did you ever think of the generations who would love Jesus because you said yes to Him? It all started when you and grandpa said yes to Jesus."

Shari would be humbled that Beth dedicated the video of her Bible study *Beloved Disciple* to her memory. On that video Beth shared that while reading Shari's studies, she felt like she knew all of her students a little bit better.

Here's one last entry from Shari's study of Beth's Bible study *A Heart Like His*:

> In the same way that David treated and accepted Mephibosheth, God does the same thing with me. He asks for me to come to Him wherever I am. He is showing me no matter what my faults and flaws, He loves me just the same. He truly is the "lover of the lame and the ultimate shame destroyer."

Why do I give you this detailed glimpse of my daughter's memorial service? To show you that she was a woman much like you! Shari had concerns as a wife and mother, all sorts of victories and defeats, and little glimpses of faith that caused her to keep seeking fellowship with God. She would be the first to tell you that she was far from perfect. Yet her life had a tremendous impact on so many people and will continue to have an impact for years to come. The full extent has yet to be shown in the lives of her daughters. God is continuing to work all things together to bring His purposes through Shari's life to fulfillment; and He is doing the same thing in you right now if you will run to Him and press in close with all of your questions, fears, challenges and victories. I guarantee you will hear His voice as you dialogue with Him.

LEAVING A LEGACY

Your legacy of faith begins the day you say yes to Jesus. The first yes is to accept His sacrifice on Calvary's cross for you and admit that you are a sinner who needs Christ to take over as the boss of your life. It is impossible to leave a legacy that you do not possess. If you would like to leave a legacy of faith to your children, begin today by taking these steps:

- Read and study your Bible on a regular basis.
- Find a church that teaches God's Word, and take your children there.
- Begin praying with your children on a daily basis.

Notes

1. Mercy Me, "I Can Only Imagine," *Almost There* (Nashville, TN: Word Records, 2001).
2. Fanny Crosby, "Blessed Assurance," in *The Celebration Hymnal* (n.p.: Word Music/Integrity Music, 1997), no. 572.

CHAPTER NINE

The Legacy of Laughter

If I could use only one word to describe my mom, it would be the word "fun." She was fun to be around even after sustaining great loss. My dad died when Mom was 63 years old. They had one of the best marriages I have ever seen, and I am sure that Mom missed Dad terribly. After my dad went to heaven, I could tell by the way she lived that Mom trusted God with the remainder of her life. She did not for one minute expect life to be dull and boring. She passed that legacy on to me.

Mom shared many fun stories about her childhood, but one of the most humorous was how she and her friends would let themselves into her dad's store at night. They would "borrow" musical instruments from the store, play them all evening and return them to the store before going home. People who bought the musical instruments never knew they had been used!

She told another story about being out in the country with friends one night and getting sprayed by a skunk. As she went through her parent's bedroom, both her parents jumped up screaming for her to go back outside!

My mom was really outrageous, and she far surpassed me when it came to having fun. After my dad died, their friends would wait to go on vacation until Mom was available to go with them. They knew that Mom brought the fun to any gathering.

Mom had some friends who lived in the condominium complex where she lived, and they played cards until midnight almost every night until my mom was 87 years old. Since Mom had severe arthritis, which made it difficult for her to walk, the three ladies came to her house to play cards. It was a common occurrence for Mom's best friend, Mary Elizabeth, to jump up at 9:00 P.M. and make a pie for the group. One of the ladies would say, "I sure would like a piece of pie," and that was Mary Elizabeth's cue to get busy making it.

There are so many stories about Mom's fun-loving nature. She said to me on many occasions, "Don't let them tell any of those stories at my funeral!" Well, Carolyn O'Neal was one of the people who spoke at my mom's memorial service, and she just had to tell a couple of stories about Mom. There was the Sunday School overnight retreat when Carolyn was awakened by loud laughter. She got up and went into one of the bedrooms to find my mom and Mary Elizabeth sitting up in bed entertaining a group of women. Both Mom and Mary Elizabeth were in their 80s at the time and definitely the oldest women in the class. (Mom didn't want to be in a Sunday School class with women her age. She called the oldest class the "On to Glory" class, and she wasn't ready for that one just yet.)

Carolyn also told about when my mom made a chocolate nativity one Christmas. She had plastic molds for the entire nativity set, complete with a chocolate stable. After Christmas was over, Mom didn't know what to do with the nativity, so she decided to eat it. She ate a part of it every day when she would walk by the buffet, where it was sitting. She started with the stable and worked her way through all the animals to the wise men, shepherds and Mary and Joseph. Then, only the baby Jesus and the manger were left. She ate the manger, but several days went by with the chocolate baby still lying on her buffet. Well, you know what happened the next day—she couldn't resist just a little more chocolate, and the last item in the nativity set was gone!

My daughter Shari certainly received the legacy of laughter that my mom had passed on to me. After Shari died, a friend of hers from high school called to say that she and Shari had lost contact over the years, but she could still hear Shari's laugh whenever she thought of her. Shari had the most distinctive laugh, and it made everyone around her laugh with her.

Cara shares some stories about her mom's legacy of laughter.

Cara Symank

*He will yet fill your mouth with laughter and
your lips with shouts of joy.*
JOB 8:21

Houston's near-tropical climate attracts a lot of bugs and critters. My mother was absolutely terrified of roaches—horrified! Before cell phones became incredibly popular, my father carried a pager. Every time my mother saw a roach, she would page him, adding the numbers 911 to the end of our phone number. She would do so to let him know he had better get home to kill it! The 911 pages became frequent until one day when my father decided it was time to put an end to this particular habit of hers.

My father said to her, "Shari, listen! From now on, I don't want to be paged with 911 unless someone is bleeding! But if you have something that you feel is an emergency and it can wait for me to get to a phone, add 922 instead of 911. I never know if something is actually wrong or not!"

From then on, he had more pages containing 922 than he knew what to do with. Thank goodness my father has as much patience as he does; it came in handy with my mother from time to time.

One day, my mom discovered my one-year-old cousin sitting in a corner at our home chewing on a dead roach. Despite my mother's nurturing character and her desire to give up anything for a child, pulling the roach from my cousin Carl's mouth would simply have been asking too much. However, she didn't leave him without help. My mother immediately began screaming for his mother, Lisa, to retrieve the roach from Carl's mouth.

There was one night about four years ago, however, when something scared her far worse than any roach ever had. We were living out in Chappell Hill on 15 acres, with no other houses in sight. That particular night my mother was sitting in the living room reading; it was a little past midnight. My sister Amanda had fallen asleep with a very high fever, and my mother was worried. She decided that she would stay downstairs a little longer, while my father was upstairs getting ready for bed. Suddenly, my mother looked up to see two green glowing eyes looking in at her through the window of the front door.

Without uttering a sound, my mother sprinted from the couch to the staircase, which led to her and my father's bedroom. Although she was silent, the sound of her stomping up the stairs was enough to frighten my father, as well as awaken Amanda. Momma ran into the bathroom where my father was and closed the door behind her.

With eyes wide open and full of tears, she began to point in the direction of the living room. My father began to panic.

"Shari, what is wrong? Shari! You have to tell me what is wrong!"

She only stood there and continued to point.

"Shari, I don't understand," my father said, attempting to move past my mother in order to find what was troubling her.

As he made his way to the bathroom door, my mother blocked the door and let out a loud, "You can't go out there! Don't do it, Jeff! Don't go out there!"

Upon seeing her reaction, my father became very upset himself. He feared that Amanda had stopped breathing, since she had been very sick earlier that night.

"Shari! What is it?" he yelled.

Still crying, my mother began to motion with her fingers the shape of the slanted green eyes. Then came the words "Martians, Jeff! Martians!"

My father walked over to the closet and pulled out his shotgun. As he was walking over to his dresser to get the shotgun shells, he began to think, *This is just great! Either way, I lose. There is either an alien on my porch or my wife has gone crazy. Either way, I am done for.*

As he made his way toward the staircase, my mother wailed, "Don't go down there, Jeff! Please don't do it!"

Doing his best to block out the sound of my mother's plea, my father quietly moved down the staircase with his shotgun in hand. As he turned the corner, there came Amanda, eyes wide with horror as she focused on the shotgun my father held. He gave Amanda a pat on the back and told her to go see her mother.

When my father reached the front door, he saw nothing. He was beginning to feel crazy for having gone downstairs—and with a shotgun of all things. He walked over to the couch where he knew my mother had been sitting and gazed out the window of the front door. Then he saw them: two green eyes. The green "eyes" she had seen in the window were a reflection of the lights that had been recently installed under the kitchen cabinets.

From that night on, anytime any of us needed a good laugh, we would give my mother a hard time about the night she saw a martian. My father told all of our relatives, leaving room for everyone to join in on the fun. We still get an enormous kick out of it every now and then. Hands down, the martian story wins the most laughs when it comes to sharing funny stories about my mother. I can find no better way to sum her up than to put it simply: She was a "mess." I heard her use that expression to describe me on several occasions; I figure she had it coming.

I hope our reminiscences about our moms will inspire you to leave the legacy of laughter to your children. Laughter, after all, is a miracle medicine for the soul. When we laugh at our shortcomings, we give our loved ones permission to laugh at their own mishaps and failures. The ability to laugh easily is a winsome trait that can help to ease life's more difficult situations.

LEAVING A LEGACY

If you would like to have more laughter as part of your relationship with your daughter, try the following ideas:

- Use laughter to lighten the next tense situation between you and your daughter. (You can always find some humor if you look for it.)
- Laugh at yourself, instead of beating yourself up, when you make a mistake.
- Find funny situations to laugh about with your daughter, and turn them into code words that only the two of you understand.

CHAPTER TEN

A Legacy Under Fire

A legacy comes under fire during hard times, such as when a daughter becomes caregiver to her mom, or when she faces the death of a loved one. The good news is that the legacy can and will survive even the most difficult circumstances. We have proof of how strong the legacy is as we are able to walk through the fire.

I guess the most lasting legacy my mom left me was to teach me how to grow old gracefully and how to die. Mom lived with me the last two-and-a-half years of her life. Even though she was confined to a wheelchair and needed someone to bathe and dress her each day, she never complained or felt sorry for herself. Instead, she grew even sweeter. She always said thank-you for everything done for her. She loved being with family and enjoyed every visitor who came. I have heard that as we age we become more of whatever we already are. Watching my mom's response to her invalidism caused me to ask God to make me sweet now so that I will be a joy to my own children if they need to care for me.

When Shari was killed, one of my greatest heartbreaks was that I wasn't able to tell Mom so that she could understand. She didn't know that Shari was gone and wasn't able to grieve with me. At the same time, I was grateful that she didn't have to endure the pain we were all going through. For the last year of Mom's life, it was almost as if she was in a fog, not seeing anything clearly. When I look back, I realize that keeping her from knowing how bad her life had become was a gift from God.

When I could no longer physically care for my mom, I was forced to find outside help. I was determined to keep her at home. I tried to hire live-in help but to no avail. I simply couldn't find anyone physically strong enough to lift Mom after she was unable to help with her transfers to and from her wheelchair. I was heartbroken as I searched for a care facility. I didn't want a large nursing home where there would be staff changes every eight hours. God's goodness and mercy led me to a personal-care home owned by a Christian woman.

I took two weeks away from work to find the place for mom to live. I spent part of that time in tears as I put her name on everything she was going to take with her: her clothes, her CD player, her pillow. When the day came for the move, my daughter Lisa was with me. She and I had already decorated Mom's room, hanging her pictures so that it might seem a little more like home. I was a total wreck by this time, and as we prepared to go pick up Mom and bring her back to her new home, I started to sob. Monaco Collins, the precious lady who owned the home, hugged me tightly and said, "Carole, I will love her like she is my own mom." Her words comforted me greatly, yet I was torn by the fact that I had not yet told Mom about the move. I also felt like I was giving up part of my responsibility as her daughter.

Precious Lisa said to me, "Mom, I'll take her."

After Lisa left in the car with Mom, I went down on the pier where Johnny and my daughter-in-law were sitting, and I just sobbed. While I sat on the swing next to Johnny, the Lord began to speak quietly to my heart, saying things like, "Haven't I taken care of your mom every day since your dad died? Do you really think I will stop taking care of her just because she is no longer in your home?" By the time Lisa returned home, I was at peace.

Not by chance, the Lord had given Lisa just the right words to say while in the car. She told Mom, "I'm taking you to stay with a friend of Momma's and mine. She is going to take care of you while Momma is traveling so much this summer." Lisa was amazed when Mom looked over and said pleasantly, "That's nice."

As I have thought back on that horrendous time in my life, I realize that I needed those two awful weeks to grieve the letting go of my mom's care. God let me cry and grieve for two solid weeks; but on the day of the move, He put His arms around me and comforted me just like a parent comforts a hurting child.

For the last seven months of Mom's life, I watched her continue to be gracious and thankful, even though she didn't know the people who were taking care of her. Most days I was devastated after visiting Mom, because she barely knew me, until one day God showed me that some of the other people in the home did know me, and I could show His love to them when I visited.

Christmas 2002 at the home was especially sad for me, and I vividly remember how a suggestion from my friend Kay Smith taught me an extremely valuable lesson that year. Our staff had made a trip to Harwin Street in Houston to look for Christmas gifts. Harwin is a street that has discount stores from one end of it to the other. One store had nothing but Christmas jewelry, and Kay purchased a huge number of bracelets just because they were such a bargain. Pat and I, on the other hand, were so overwhelmed by the store full of jewelry that we went back to the car and waited until the others finished shopping.

On Saturday morning, as Kay and I were preparing to go visit my mom, Kay said to me, "Why don't you take some Christmas bracelets to the ladies at the home today?" She continued, "I certainly have more than I need." I was thrilled to be able to purchase some of the bracelets, and we had a great time putting one on the arm of each of the ladies and leaving some for their caretakers.

Every time I visited after that, one elderly lady who lived at the home with her 50-year-old daughter, who was severely afflicted with cerebral palsy, would make a point to thank me for the beautiful bracelet. She always said, "Thank you for being so kind to us." God used Kay to teach me that God can use our simplest actions to minister His love to others.

Even though the mother-daughter legacy passed down to me was under fire, and I was miserable about not having my mom with me in my own home, God used that time to teach me that a legacy is about life. Living out our legacy when it is under fire shows us how tenderly our God loves us, because He will walk with us through the fire each step of the way.

Visits to Mom became so much easier when I was able to pass on to others the legacy of love given to me by my precious mom. Even after Mom didn't know my name, I knew she knew who I was, because each time

I entered her room she said, "Well, darlin'!" Although her mind was almost gone, her love for me never wavered.

The last three months of Mom's life were filled with hospice nurses. Every nurse I met who cared for Mom was a professing Christian. I was continually amazed at God's watchful care over my mom until the minute He took her home. When that time came, God was so precious to allow my daughter Lisa to be with Mom. The night Shari died, Lisa had been at the farm and was unable to be with the rest of us at the hospital. Lisa and Shari had been so close and did almost everything together. Being with Mom when she took her last breath gave Lisa the closure she had not received when Shari had been taken from her so abruptly.

I returned from California the afternoon of my mom's death. Lisa had taken care of everything—she had even choosen the casket and filled out all the paperwork. I wrote Mom's obituary for the newspaper on the plane trip home, and all that was left to do was take Mom's clothes to the funeral home and sign the paperwork. It was a great comfort to me to see Mom's loving legacy shine forth in Lisa during this time of grief.

I am sure that you have had opportunities to see the fruit of your mother's legacy in your life. Those tests occurred without warning and often during difficult circumstances, didn't they? It is impossible to study, or cram, for life's tests. How you handle them depends on what has been poured into you, beginning in childhood, and on how the Lord has matured that legacy in you. Now doesn't that stir strong feelings in you about the importance of how you interact with your daughter every single day?! For she, too, will be tested at the most inopportune and surprising moments—and sometimes those tests will contain much pain and grief. How your daughter handles those seasons of testing will depend a great deal on what you have been pouring into her during the most ordinary moments of daily life.

If you are childless or single, these words are for you, too. You influence more children than you probably realize in your roles as aunt, neighbor, friend, Sunday School teacher, volunteer worker, children's choir leader and more. If the girls in your sphere of influence have not been given a loving legacy by their moms, then your input can help to instill strength and stability into their future.

LEAVING A LEGACY

What is happening in your life right now? Are you at a point where your legacy is under fire? If you are a

Christian, you can rejoice in the fact that the fire will not consume you and that this trial will polish your life like fine gold. Fire refines the legacy. When we persevere through fiery trials, others can see the power of God at work in our lives and also find inspiration and comfort for their own trials. Scripture teaches us that hard times develop perseverance that leads to maturity (see Jas. 1:2). If your legacy is under fire right now, try the following ideas and see what changes take place in your heart:

- Thank God for loving you in the midst of the fire.
- Ask God to turn the flame of your own fire from white-hot to a warm glow that ministers to those around you.
- Reach out to others who are walking through the fire after you have come out of yours (see 2 Cor. 3:3-4).

CHAPTER ELEVEN

The Legacy of Loss

While some people are prone to brood and complain about their lot in life, my mom was quite the opposite. After my dad died in 1976, I watched as Mom faced life without him. One day she told me that her habit was to get up every morning and ask, "Lord, what wonderful thing do You have for me today?" She trusted God with her days, and He came through for her. Losing Dad was just the first of Mom's losses. Eight months later, her oldest and closest sister, Irene, died of cancer.

I watched Mom as she battled breast cancer in her 70s and had both breasts removed. She never complained and always had the most upbeat attitude.

I also observed Mom weather the loss of my sister, Glenda, who died in 1994. I called my sister Sissy because I couldn't say the word "Glenda" as a baby. Sissy had never been sick in her life, and the only time she was ever hospitalized was for the births of her three children. It was so devastating for our entire family to watch a perfectly healthy woman lose her speech following a major stroke. For Sissy's sixtieth birthday, we had planned to go to her home to celebrate. She had just come home from the hospital the day before, and my mom had spent the day with her. The morning of her birthday, Sissy didn't wake up— she had suffered a massive stroke during the night. Sissy spent the last three weeks of her life in a coma. My elderly mom's love and care for my sister in those last three months of Sissy's life after the first stroke were a legacy I never expected to be repeated in my own lifetime. My mom said to me after Sissy died, "Parents should never have to outlive their children." I didn't truly understand the significance of her words until I was called to give up my Shari.

Here are some of Cara's journal entries from the months after Shari's death. She wrote with transparency and complete honesty, never intending her journal entries to be read by others. But she is grateful for the opportunity to reveal the thoughts that a grieving child has when no one is watching or putting a value on them.

Cara Symank

In this you greatly rejoice, though now for a little while you may have had to suffer grief in all kinds of trials. These have come so that your faith—of greater worth than gold, which

perishes even though refined by fire—may be proved
genuine and may result in praise, glory and honor
when Jesus Christ is revealed.

1 PETER 1:6-7

February 18, 2002

I have not forgotten—I just haven't stopped going and going. I feel a crash coming up. Although I have test after test and paper after paper, I'm just going to stop and think and spend time with God. Today was just one of those days—the kind where you want to crawl back in bed and then get out and start all over. I was thinking about what happened over and over again, and I just couldn't seem to make any sense of it. I kept thinking, *No, Mom's at home. She's at home with the girls. She's at home talking stupid (talking stupid?) to the dogs. She's at home not cleaning but pretending to anyway. She's at home sitting in her chair, drinking coffee and doing her Bible study. Yeah, that sounds right! That's where Mom is.* But then I kept seeing her lying there in the yard. I just see the whole thing. It's such a small view. The red Expedition—then the orange tape—then Mom lying there between the red Expedition, the orange tape and that one tree that now has a car in it. There was such a dark sky behind that scene. Then my thoughts began to torment me: *Mom isn't at home, and she's not in the front yard either. Then where is she? Heaven. Yeah, that's right; but she should be at home. But she was in the yard—that's where I saw her. Oh, I almost forgot the cruelty of that dreaded casket. You know, when I had to go see her. They made me go because they said I would regret it later if I didn't. Her chin. All I can think about is what they did to her chin. Why did it look so . . . long and just not right? It wasn't even her. I don't remember anything but her chin. Oh, yeah, and her gold sweater. Why did we get gold? It clashed with, well, everything now. That wasn't even her.* Those were my thoughts. They just come and they don't make sense, even to me. How could I ever explain this to anyone else? "Um, yes, counselor, I am 19, but I am having a hard time grasping the concept that my mom isn't lying in the front yard anymore." The counselor would probably just ask me to repeat myself, hoping I had said something else—anything but that.

November 20, 2002

I don't really feel like writing today, but then again, I haven't really felt like writing any day. In two days it will be a year without Mom. When I force myself to think about it, the atmosphere of that night comes right back to me. It was so dark, damp and cold. It seemed like people suddenly swarmed like ants. I pushed one guy away and told him that he had probably killed my mom. I later found him and apologized. That night God knew what He was doing. I just wish I didn't have to live life without my mom in order for others to learn about Christ. It doesn't feel fair, but I have to remember that God is just. When I think about it, it's like I'm sitting back and watching it all over again as if it were on a big-screen TV. I can see myself leaning down in her puddle of blood to tell her one last time that I love her. Who would have ever thought? Not many people know how a moment like that feels. I bet she heard me though. I probably know the look that she had on her face as she lay there facedown in the yard. I bet she was gritting her teeth. I bet she was listening but was unable to respond. I hope she knew that I loved her.

December 25, 2002

I want Mom back so badly that I can hardly stand it. Dad tries really hard, and he's absolutely amazing. Mom set the stakes high for us girls when she chose my dad. We'll all be lucky if we get someone that good. It's just that Mom wasn't here today, but she never is. The emptiness is unbearable. The silence is even more unbearable. Everyone thinks about her, everyone hurts, but no one talks. I can feel it in my gut. I can't bear the pain anymore. It is so empty without Mom. I am so upset for Dad, because the one person he loves so deeply, he can't touch. And for the girls: It's hard for me to tread through the pain, but what is it like to be in their place? All of a sudden, life is in slow motion, nothing is in the right spot. We don't celebrate holidays like we used to; no one cares to celebrate like before. We aren't even doing Christmas with Dad's side of the family until Sunday. Will the gutlessness end? Mom was the life of all these events. She laughed, she planned and she wanted everything to be perfect. She made things so right. Dad does all he can to make us feel like nothing has changed, but it has. Is this what kids of divorce feel like? I want my momma so bad. I feel like crying like a baby until she comes back, although she won't. I really can't handle this pain. Why not? I feel like all of a sudden I have reached this place, and it's like I have to remind myself to breathe. I'm not being dramatic. I honestly wish I knew how to stop the pain from barreling me over.

April 20, 2003

Today was Easter. I am at a place where I feel at a loss for words. People spend way too much time talking rather than listening. Today was so . . . odd. I just have a lack of words these days. It's weird. There is emotion—I just can't voice it. Sometimes I feel like I am just aimlessly watching others and feeling as if I have lost the ability to speak. Then again, Dad gave me so much opportunity to talk tonight and I didn't say anything, because I don't know what there is to say. So strange. I don't know. I am going to go call Jim Bob, because today was his first Easter without his dad, and I remember wanting someone to call and check on me when I went through all the "firsts" without Mom. I am going to do for him what I wanted most. I'll probably be back to write more later.

My granddaughter's journal entries underscore that those of us who are called to the legacy of loss join a club we would just as soon not join; but I can say with a sense of gratefulness that when another person experiences pain like ours, we can identify immediately and our hearts go out to that person. No one can truly empathize with another person's pain until he or she has been through the legacy of loss. If you know someone who is hurting from a loss right now, consider how you can show that person love. Here are some suggestions:

- Call or write to see how he or she is doing—continue to call or write weeks or months after the loss, when other cards and calls have ceased.
- Mail a card with a personal note inside. It's always a comfort for the one grieving to know that someone else remembers the loved one. Add an anecdote or something special about the person.
- Give a memorial gift in honor of the loved one.

CHAPTER TWELVE

The Legacy of Acceptance

Life has a way of leveling the playing field through the losses we experience, both great and small. I am convinced that we cannot become the people God wants us to become unless we learn to accept what we cannot change.

I can see God's hand today in so many areas that concern the time surrounding the loss of Shari. In October, just one month before Shari died, she took a trip to North Carolina with me. She had a burning desire to go with me, and I'm sure she thought it was because she wanted to see our friend Jan Jarrett and also because she and Jeff longed to one day move to North Carolina. I am convinced that God gave us those three days because it would be our last trip together and because God is just plain good to His kids.

The first Christmas without Shari was excruciating for all of us. She had bought a placemat in North Carolina for her cat's food bowl and had wrapped it beautifully. The card read, "From the one who feeds you." She also wrapped a package of mix to make homemade dog biscuits for her two golden retrievers, and on top of the package were cookie cutters in the shape of bones. All of it was so Shari.

All during the holidays I had been with Shari's girls. I observed Cara as she endeavored to buy the exact wrapping paper her mom would have liked. I'm sure she spent so much time on this type of thing because she felt that she had to be both mom and sister to Christen and Amanda. Jeff and all three of the girls began a new life that first Christmas, and it wasn't the life they had planned. I am convinced today more than ever that our God doesn't take it lightly when His children suffer.

I am trusting God to make up to Jeff and those girls in millions of ways for having lost their wife and mom so soon. God knew before Shari ever took her first breath the day and the hour she would go home to be with Him. My job now is to trust God with today and all of our tomorrows. In Him I place my trust! My prayer is that my faith in God's goodness will be a lasting legacy after I am gone.

I treasure the last picture Shari took of Christen after Christen had caught a flounder. Because Shari was homeschooling Christen and Amanda, she was able to bring them to the bay and stay with my mom when I needed to go to California with Johnny for his medical appointments. The picture was taken in October and was on a roll of film I had developed after Shari was gone. Christen was smiling shyly as she held that big flounder, and as I looked at the picture, I was reminded once again of the joy that Shari had found in being a mom.

My prayer as you read these words is that you will not take your God-given role of mother for granted. I know there have been many times when I did a really poor job of mothering, always reasoning that I would do better the next day. But today is all we know. May we make each day the best day possible for the people we love. May we be the best wives, the best moms, the best friends and the best daughters that we can be—*today*. This day, as you read, is a wonderful present from God.

By God's mercy, Cara has begun to learn the legacy of acceptance much earlier than most of us. That lesson came to a head one day when her desire for life to return to the way it used to be overwhelmed her and she wanted to give up her journal writing. Here's the way Cara described her breakthrough moment:

Cara Symank

The moment when I must leave to return to school always bothers me, because I struggle with feelings of helplessness toward my family when I am away from home. Occasionally, my feelings become too overwhelmingly painful. It is at those times that I find myself having a long talk with my father before I am able to feel somewhat at peace.

I am used to helping others, yet I am unable to easily accept the willingness of others to help carry me along when my burden is too heavy. I struggle, as most do, with wanting to be seen as strong rather than one who experiences fragile emotions from time to time. However, I am learning that "perfect" is not necessarily a good thing to be. If you really stop to think about the kind of person you most respect, it will most likely be someone who willingly admits faults, weaknesses and struggles.

Last night, while speaking to my father, I told my dad through tears, "I cannot continue writing. I have moments when I get so upset and I cannot see the good in our situation." My father responded, "What is the point if you leave out the difficult moments? Christians tend to have a skewed perception these days, believing that they are doing one another a favor by portraying a life devoid of weaknesses and struggles. How can we encourage one another and meet others' needs if everyone falls for Satan's deception that those who are truly Christians live lives free of heartache and trials? Why not write about every aspect of grief?"

My dad's words reminded me of the vitality of being transparent. Somewhere along the way I had become entangled in Satan's lie and had grasped the

false need to be seen as one who has everything together all of the time.

The legacy of acceptance is an important legacy to pass down to our children. This legacy doesn't negate or bypass the necessity of expressing all that we are feeling. Expressing fear, anger, grief and other feelings is a natural and healthy part of getting to the point of acceptance.

Time, as well, truly is the great healer. While I live on this earth, I will continue to miss my dad, my mom, my sister and my daughter Shari; but the raw pain diminishes with the passing of time, and the memories grow more precious with each passing day.

The legacy of acceptance isn't only about the loss of a loved one. All of us, at some time, will experience grief through losses both great and small—the loss of a job, the loss of a prized possession, the loss of a friendship, of a marriage, of our health, of our youth, of our reputation. *Loss* is something all of us will experience and strive to get through. The inexorable losses we experience provide all the more reason to model the legacy of acceptance in front of our children and in front of those children with whom we have influence.

When we can accept the truth that a loss has left a huge void in our lives, we can begin to experience the legacy of acceptance and see it flicker into flame.

LEAVING A LEGACY

Have you experienced a loss in your life that you are still unable to accept? If so, maybe today is the day God would have you enter into your legacy of acceptance. Here's what you can do to begin:

- Write every day for 30 minutes about your loss. Don't edit your thoughts—be as brutally honest as you need to be to avoid suppressing any emotions that could hinder your healing.
- Ask God to bring peace to your heart as you accept your loss.
- Watch expectantly for the dark clouds to lift from your heart, and thank God when they do. A grateful heart is the key to joy in the midst of all that life sends your way.

CHAPTER THIRTEEN

A Legacy Revealed

I took six weeks off from work after Shari's death. There was not much going on because of the holidays, and I would not have accomplished much had I been at work. I returned on January 6 in such a quandary. I had what looked like a million e-mails and a manuscript deadline of January 20 for the devotional book *Today Is the First Day*. But God came through for me in might and power, and I wrote my entire part of the book in eight days! After completing the manuscript, I was convinced that nothing is too hard for God and that our family was going to be all right.

During that time, Cara was due to move into the dorm at Texas A&M to start the spring semester as a new student. The morning she moved, our staff was having prayer together, and I exclaimed, "How is Cara going to get the emotional help she needs at Texas A&M?! She's never been away from home, and the grief is still so raw." Nancy Taylor, who works with me in First Place, said, "Let's pray that God provides a friend for Cara who has had a loss like hers."

Before that day was over, Cara called me and said, "Mimi, you are not going to believe the miracle that has happened." When you read Cara's account of that day, you will understand how I knew that God was not taking our loss lightly and that He was going to make good what Satan had intended for evil. I knew that the legacy God began was going to continue on.

Cara Symank

My roommate had not yet arrived at school my first night in the dorm, but one of my suite mates, Katy, was there awaiting my arrival. My father and my sisters came up to the room and gave me good-bye hugs. Before they left, I led them into Katy's room and introduced them, and then nervously I watched them depart. Katy and I stood, staring at each other. There was a short moment of silence, and then Katy said, with a great burst of excitement, "So tell me about your family!" Of all the questions I could have been confronted with at that moment, those words were definitely ones that I did not want to hear. In fact, they caused my heart to fall into the pit of my stomach. After a moment, I hesitantly replied, "Well, that was my family, all of them. I don't have a mom." My head was pounding faster than my heart. I had just told her that I did not have a mom. *What on earth am I thinking*, I said to myself. *Am I trying to pretend that I never had a mother in the first place?*

I looked up to see Katy's mouth fall wide open as she shouted, "I don't have a momma either!" There was a defining moment of silence as we stared directly at one another. Finally, we each explained the unexpected loss of a mother in the year 2001. Katy's mother had simply gone to the hospital one morning for a blood transfusion and had passed away with no sign of illness or warning. Although I felt deep sympathy for the pain Katy had experienced and was still experiencing, I thanked God for hand delivering me to someone who fully understood what it meant to suddenly lose a mother. Even in the midst of my great sorrow, I was able to praise God, because at that moment I knew more than ever before that God had His hand on our family's situation. It was a confirmation to me that He knew and that He cared.

Katy and I have spent countless hours, whether taking late night walks or driving in the car, discussing both the good memories about our mothers and the pain of losing them. I cannot imagine what greater challenges I would have faced had God not placed me with the roommates I was given. Along with Katy, I was placed with Ashley and Lori. All are Christian girls. Ashley's vivaciousness overtook any part of me that felt compelled to keep to myself, while Lori's quiet spirit connected with mine. I am grateful to God for granting me discernment to hear His desire to place me in the right dorm room rather than to follow my plan to room with a friend from high school. God knew exactly what I needed to successfully ease into my first semester away from home at such a tender time in my life.

Along with Katy came two of her friends from Eastland High School—Michael and Jim Bob. Both are great Christian guys with outstanding character. The six of us immediately became very close, always finding ways to spend time together. Unfortunately, Jim Bob's father, who was a preacher, became ill with cancer at the age of 49 and passed away in October 2002, shortly after being diagnosed. Despite the devastation of our situations, God's sovereignty showed itself once again as He allowed each of us who had lost a parent to have one another for support. God knew the pain that each of us would face long before it happened, and He chose to give us the comfort of one another's friendship rather than letting us hurt individually.

Jim Bob and I have now had the opportunity to discuss my mother and his father and the struggles we have faced as a result of their deaths. We are confident that though there are many aspects of our situations that we will never understand, we will make it through, having developed stronger character as a result. I remain in awe of God's faithfulness to ensure that Katy, Jim Bob and I have support while away at school. Not only do we have each other, friends who understand the pain of grieving a parent's death, but we were also blessed with friends such as Michael, Ashley and Lori, as well as others, who have faithfully encouraged us and who have been determined to keep us all smiling.

The spring semester of 2003 was also brutally challenging. Early on Saturday morning, one week after beginning classes, I received a phone call and was told that Katy's sister, Becca—her only sibling—had been killed in a car accident at the young age of 22. Although it breaks my heart to say this, at that time most of us in our circle of friends lost hope and questioned God. Thankfully, each and every one of us quickly began talking with one another, and we were able to regain faith and realize that God is a just and almighty God. He has undoubtedly placed each of us where we are for a specific reason.

A short time after my arrival at Texas A&M University, I became accustomed to phone calls from my father that began, "Cara, I have something to tell you. I believe this is just one of those things." He would start out with those words every time he had experienced something that he felt was miraculous.

At the time of my mom's death, my family and I had been living in Chappell Hill, Texas, where we were in the process of building a house. Chappell Hill is approximately one hour from Houston, where the majority of our family lives. We moved out to Chappell Hill unexpectedly just five months prior to Thanksgiving, because our home in Houston had flooded. After my mother's death, we decided to return to Houston to be close to other family members. Now my father was an hour away from the house he was constructing.

I can only imagine the dilemma my father faced at that time. He had to be "enough parent" to be both mom and dad to three girls, while working in Houston and, in his "spare time," making frequent trips out to Chappell Hill to work on the house. The amazing thing is that I do not recall him ever wavering or acting as if it were too big a task for him to handle. Despite his own heartache, he continued to work while keeping extremely late night hours when one of his children needed his help to grieve.

As a result of the accident, we were each given a specific amount of money from the insurance company.

After much careful thought, my dad considered quitting his job and finishing the house with the money we had each received. He reasoned that this would allow him to have more time to assist us in any way needed, while using the money to invest in the house. My dad would put the house on the market once it was built, and he would give back to each of us the money we originally had received. Although the idea seemed reasonable, he worried that he would make a wrong decision and put our family into further trouble.

On Good Friday 2002, my father stopped by the cemetery and simply began praying. He asked for a clear answer concerning the decision about his working situation and the house. When he had finished praying, he walked to his vehicle, still feeling unsure of the right thing to do.

Upon opening the door of the vehicle, his cell phone rang. It was a woman who introduced herself as an attorney for Christen and Amanda. She explained that she had been appointed to them to ensure that they would not receive their checks from the insurance company until the age of 18. Rather than feeling shock at this news, my father immediately recognized that this was his answer to prayer. He was not to quit his job, and he was confident that there was another plan, a better plan.

Only a very short time passed before this better plan appeared. On the following Thursday, a partner of the company he was working for approached him and inquired about the progress of our family and the house during our time of loss. My father briefly explained the difficulty of the situation. The very next day, only one week after his prayer for a clear answer, the partners of his company requested his presence in the corporate office. There he was told that the leaders of the company had unanimously decided to help him out in any way possible. They felt it was appropriate to give him paid leave until he had finished building the house. They also would loan him whatever money he needed to complete the building process. In addition, my father was going to be able to keep his company vehicle and phone.

Though my father had faith that we would be taken care of, never in his wildest dreams did he imagine that God was going to provide a miracle of this magnitude. When he called to tell me about it, I could detect a great deal of joy and peace in the midst of his brokenness as he spoke the words, "Cara, I have something to tell you. I believe this is just one of those things."

Every daughter comes to a point in life when she realizes that the baton is being passed to her from her mom. One of those times came for me after my dad died, just before Thanksgiving in 1976. My mom, who had always had all the holiday meals at her home, never cooked another holiday meal. That first Thanksgiving without my dad began a new legacy, and I was amazed that Johnny and I were up to the task. We had Thanksgiving and Christmas at our home that year and every year following.

I believe that Cara felt a baton had been passed to her last summer as she was in the middle of writing this book. She came into my office most days to write so that she could focus. On one particular day, I had a lunch appointment, and Cara said she was going to stay in the office and write. It was a gloomy day, and I guess that after I left for lunch, Cara's plans changed. It had been a year and a half since Shari's death, and I believe God prompted her to do something significant during lunch. She took a bold step and faced life without her mom. As you read Cara's words about the silence of that day, maybe you will think about the day your mom passed the baton to you. It was probably the day you got the first peek at the legacy you were to receive.

Cara Symank

This morning as I was preparing to make the trip into Houston where I would write for the day, my mind wandered while seeking to find a thought on which to write. As I stood alone in the bathroom and heard nothing, it immediately hit me: It was the silence that had bothered me the most. I spontaneously decided to visit the cemetery, which I had only done once before, more than a year ago, with my father and my sister Christen. This time I was on my own.

When I turned the corner and the cemetery came into view, I focused my eyes on the entrance to the grounds. It was raining, just as it was on the day we had to place my mother's body in the ground. I drove past. *I cannot go without flowers,* I thought. *Why am I going to go if I do not have anything to take?*

I drove to the store and picked out the best roses, and then went back to the cemetery. I was playing a praise-and-worship CD as loud as I could. As I drove inside the gate, my eyes fixed on row after row of colored headstones. I drove to the far end of the cemetery but remained in the car. I continued to stare at the endless rows of headstones as I carefully removed the paper from around the roses. A jumble of thoughts came into my mind. *Should I keep a rose for myself? What do I want one of these roses for? It might be nice to have a rose from the bundle that I brought out here. That is a really strange thought; I am not going to keep a rose.* As I lifted the roses and glanced down to the seat where they had been lying, there remained a single rose that somehow had never made it out of the plastic wrap. I was supposed to keep a rose after all. I smiled at the clearness of the answer to such a small and meaningless question.

As I continued to listen to the CD, I thought, *If I leave the door open, it would not be quiet out there. There would not be anything disrespectful about playing rather loud praise music out here. After all, I hope that is what most of these people are actually doing in heaven anyway.* Despite my ability to rationalize my desire to leave my car door open, I made the decision to get out and close the door behind me.

I walked to the general area in which I vaguely remembered my mother being buried and looked for the tree stump to the left of where she was placed. We had not yet put a headstone on her grave. Once my eyes were fixed on the tree stump that had been freshly cut at the time of her burial, I was startled by the thought, *Oh my gosh, I am standing on top of her!* I quickly moved to the side, just to hear my next thought, *Well, great, now I am standing on someone else.* I found humor in the abrupt thoughts that broke the silence.

There I stood, flowers in hand, staring at the ground. I continued to look down for only a few moments before gazing off once again at the rows of gray stone. *Well, I am here,* I thought. *I am not sure what I'm doing here. My mom is not even here. What am I doing here?* In accordance with the silence, I quietly set the roses on the grass. *Well, they look really bad right there,* I thought to myself. For a moment I attempted to scatter them around differently, hoping to make them look somewhat better. My attempt was in vain, because they looked just as horrible as ever.

When I walked to the car, what a relief it was to open my car door to the sounds of praise. Suddenly I realized that the silence had bothered me so much because in that large cemetery where I stood alone in what I thought was complete stillness, I was in fact the only one who was silent. Today my mother is not silent at all. In fact, she is singing praises to the Lord as I stand in silence longing to hear those words and that music.

LEAVING A LEGACY

I was 34 years old when my dad died; Cara was 19 when her mom was taken. Losing a parent is always a clear sign of the passing of a legacy. Sometimes we don't accept the baton passed to us from our parents because of grief or anger at the situation. Some people waste valuable years with their legacy hidden, because they refuse to pick up the baton and run with it. The apostle Paul said in Galatians 5:7, "You were running a good race. Who cut in on you and kept you from obeying the truth?" If you have not yet accepted the baton God is revealing as your legacy, I pray that you will take these steps:

- Thank God that you have a legacy that will live on after you are gone.
- Find someone with whom you can talk about your legacy.
- Begin today to live in such a way that you, too, will pass on a godly legacy to those within your sphere of influence.

CHAPTER FOURTEEN

A Legacy to the Generations

Show me, O Lord, my life's end and the number of my days;
let me know how fleeting is my life.

PSALM 39:4

Cara and I wrote this book about the mother-daughter legacy because we realized that since our moms were no longer with us, their legacy was now ours to pass on. And what a legacy they lived! We wanted others to know about their lives.

More important, our reflections about our moms began to stir up a mighty desire within me to help moms everywhere see the importance of living each day as if it were their last opportunity to affect the legacy they would pass on to their daughters. The more I thought of what my mom's life had meant to me, the more I became like an evangelist, preaching about the huge role a mom plays in the lives of her children. A daughter learns most of what she knows from watching her mom live.

I feel very blessed to be able to watch the legacy my two remaining children will pass on to their own children. I could write a separate book about both of them and what wonderful adults they are, as well as great parents to their children. I am so very proud of Lisa and

John and blessed beyond words to be their mom. I love Kent, Lisa's husband, and Lisa, John's wife, and I thank God for Christian spouses for my kids.

The reason for focusing exclusively on my daughter Shari and her legacy is that she no longer has the opportunity to live it out. While we are alive, we still have the chance to do a better job than we did the day before. Death's finality reveals the fruit of whatever we have lived. That truth is both sobering and energizing. *You can plant a beautiful harvest in your children by the life you now lead!*

The questions at the end of this chapter will help you to prune and nurture areas in your life that need attention. Ask these questions of yourself honestly and often. Your children will be glad you did.

Cara Symank

When I had almost completed my portion of this book, a stranger who overheard a conversation about it approached me and questioned my credentials for being able to write it. I confess that I am simply a college student with a story I felt called by God to tell. A large part of my writing has revealed the portion of my life that has been spent without my mother's presence. For it was not until her absence that I began to consider how my mother's life had impacted my own.

My mother certainly did not do everything perfectly, but she believed that it was her purpose to be the best wife, mother and woman in Christ that she could possibly be, and I genuinely believe she succeeded in all three areas.

Though at times I have been overwhelmed with sadness that my mother will not be present at my wedding or at the birth of my children or even attend my college graduation, I strive to focus on the time that she was, in fact, with me. I must force myself to remember that on the very day that I was put into my mother's arms, God knew that she would have only 7,049 days to impact my life.

My desire is to be the same kind of mother to my children that my mother was to me. I believe that will come naturally because it is what I was taught; it is the only way I know how to be.

LEAVING A LEGACY

As you ponder the legacy your mother passed to you and the one you will leave to your daughter, consider this question, *What would I do to affect that legacy if I could do it over?* The great thing about asking such a question is that as long as you are breathing, you can choose to make some changes. You can take more risks to be the woman you want to be, you can focus on what really matters in life, and you can do something that will live on after you die. Here are just a few suggestions related to those goals.

Risk More

How can you make up for time lost? It might mean relocating to live closer to your daughter. A radical thought? Maybe, but maybe not. I have an aunt and uncle who lived their entire married life in Pittsburgh, Pennsylvania, and raised their two sons there. When their youngest son was transferred to Arizona, they didn't think twice about selling their home and moving to Arizona to be near their family. When their son was transferred a second time to Texas, they picked up and moved again! Life is too short to be separated from family if we can do something about it.

Focus on What Really Matters

Consider the activities and the to-do lists that take most of your time. Are there some things you're not doing that would be extremely important to the kind of legacy you want to leave? Make a list with two columns, one labeled "Important" and the other labeled "Not Important." List all your activities in these columns. After you finish the list, pray about your life and ask God to show you which things to remove from the "Not Important" side of the list. Legacy building requires a daily concentration on what is truly important and then pouring your time into those things.

Do Something Worthwhile That Will Live On After You Die

The only parts of us that we want to live on after we are gone are the qualities written about in this book. Those qualities are essential to passing a loving legacy from mother to daughter. The following questions recap the message of this book. It would be good for you to ask these questions of yourself periodically. You might want to place copies of them in your Bible or your daily planner, or any other place where you regularly go to reflect on life and your commitments.

- Am I leaving a legacy that nurtures my family by the example I set?
- Am I giving my family not only my time but my whole self as well?
- Am I living a life rich with godly character as

evidenced by the words I speak?
- Is my life full of faith, which my daughter can watch me live out in the decisions I make?
- Would my daughter use the words "laughter" and "fun" to describe me or would those words remind her of me?
- What do I do when my legacy is under fire?
- How do I react or respond to loss?
- Do I accept or reject life's hurts and pain? Do I stay stuck, or do I move on?

Your honest answers to these questions will tell you if the legacy you want to leave will be alive and vibrant in your children after you are gone. May we each make the needed changes in our lives and our schedules today so that God can use us in the lives of our daughters.

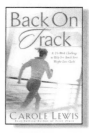